NO TEARS FOR THE CHERISHED

A Memoir

DR. NYABOKE NDUATI

NO TEARS FOR THE CHERISHED
Dr. Nyaboke Nduati

© Copyright 2023 by Dr. Nyaboke Nduati

All rights reserved. No part of this publication may be reproduced, stored in a retrieval system or transmitted in any way by means of electronic, mechanical, photocopy, recording or otherwise without the prior written permission of the Author except as provided by copyright law.

Published and distributed by:
Thousandfold Ltd
P.O. Box. 9263,
Nairobi - 00100
Kenya

www.nyabokenduati.com

Cover design and layout by:
MediaGraphics Studio
Email: desgichuru@gmail.com
Phone: +254708625252

ISBN: 978_9914_50_293_0

Disclaimer: This book is a memoir. It reflects the author's present recollections of experiences and the world she has witnessed over time. Some names, places, and characteristics have been changed, some events have been compressed, and some dialogue has been recreated. The views expressed in this memoir are solely those of the author and are a representation of her world, from her perspective.

For my beloved children
I fought this battle so you wouldn't have to.

Acknowledgments

My deep gratitude to my friend and mentor, Oliver Sabot, for inspiring me to finally write this story. His coaching on leadership and vulnerability established the firm foundation upon which I am able to stand in my authenticity and share my story with others who may need hope for the future, and a little courage to find their own voices.

Arthur Flowers - my teacher, mentor, and friend - thank you for the important role that you have played in my life over the years. Thank you for stopping to pay attention to that awkward youngster with a beat-up manuscript. You changed my life in a major way. I appreciate and honor you.

The chapters in this story had many first readers, all of whose comments and feedback helped give me the courage to continue writing, even when I was afraid. Special thanks to my friend, Robert Burale, for reminding me often that the world is ready for my story. I appreciate you showing up for me with generosity and kindness.

My friend and brother in the craft, Niq Mhlongo, thank you for your uplifting words in the early stages of this journey, which helped me believe in the power of my own story and my voice.

My friends Jackson Biko, Frey Kebede, Gillian Jakes, Muingo Mutisya, Roselyne Mutemi, Jeffrey Allen, and Patrick Wambua, thank you for taking the time to read the manuscript at various stages. Your thoughtful feedback was much appreciated throughout this process.

Major thanks to my cover and layout designer, Desmond Gichuru, for his outstanding design work.

It is never an easy task to write a memoir, and I tried hard to be kind and sensitive in my retelling of this story. Thank you to all of those beautiful humans whose stories intertwined with mine over the years. I apologize in advance if my story will upset anyone. I have nothing but love for all of you. My personal belief is that there are no complete heroes and villains in any story. We are all flawed humans doing the best that we can under different, sometimes very difficult, circumstances.

And finally, my deep appreciation for my husband, my love, who has loved me from day one and continues to love me through all the seasons of our lives. And my children, who have taught me to love unconditionally and given me reason to seek beauty in each moment. I love you infinitely and wish you a lifetime filled with an abundance of beauty, love, joy, peace, and favor.

Contents

Acknowledgments v

Chapter One 9
Chapter Two 65
Chapter Three 113
Chapter Four 157
Chapter Five 185
Chapter Six 233
Chapter Seven 257
Chapter Eight 289

CHAPTER ONE

Dear Mama,

I became you. The woman that I am today is a version of you, evolving, slowly, and sometimes painfully, as I write through the pages of my life, hoping for a different outcome. You pulled yourself out of the throngs of poverty, made a decent life for yourself, only to be broken back down by the man that you chose to love. Years of your life were spent entangled in the messy chains of domestic abuse, depression, illness, and the heartbreak of coming face-to-face with death, not knowing what will become of your children. Death came for you, hasty, impatient, and without a care for whatever trail of generational traumas it would leave behind.

Shame and silence defined much of our lives together. I learned early on that speaking up was an invitation for trouble, and that I was safer being quiet and invisible. The self-effacing followed me into adulthood, and now I struggle with my own version of the personal demons that wrestled you to the ground, turning you from the beautiful, optimistic, and joyful woman that you were, to the wounded mother that I knew. I achieved tremendous success at a young age, but deep down remains the same fear, the same shame, the same struggle with our perceived realities of who we are and what we deserve in the world.

Mama, you did the best that you could for me, but I came out of my childhood scarred and damaged. I must now fight to unlearn the lies I accepted about myself. I must let go of the self sabotaging tendencies that keep me from soaring, and prevent any sparks that flare up in my soul from blossoming beyond my self-imposed walls of limitation. Everything about my childhood told me that I was unworthy of love and success, that I was doomed to a meaningless existence. Mama, my spirit was broken before I understood anything about life. But I refused to stay broken. I could feel my brokenness, and the crippling fear that my life would not count for much, but alongside that was the persistent fire within, the deep belief that I was called for something, and that it was my responsibility to fight through whatever life threw at me in order to achieve my purpose. It was an awkward in-between space of feeling both irreversibly damaged, and highly valuable.

As a parent now, I understand that despite your best effort, your pain was too great, and your anger too consuming, to allow your beautiful heart to thrive. You bore and raised six children. You stayed as long as you could, and when your body gave in at the young age of thirty nine, you left heartbroken. For your children especially, and the uncertainty of their future. I hope that tragic as your life was, you found joy in the few years you got to spend with your children, and that you found peace on the other side. Mama, this year I am the exact same age you were when you passed on. Some nights I wake up terrified, plagued by nightmares of illness, death, and loss. My logical mind understands that I am not you. That it is unlikely you and I will both meet the same fate. But subconsciously, I struggle with the deep fear of an early demise, and the suffering of those left behind.

Your death broke me in many ways. There were times in my younger years that I believed I was broken beyond repair. I lived with a persistent dull ache in my chest. Sometimes when I got overly anxious about something, the pain intensified. But it was always there, a constant reminder that something was not right. Mama, I prayed for a fresh start. I did not think my heart could be salvaged.

I cannot tell you how many books and articles on wellness I've read, how many podcasts, videos, and documentaries I have watched trying to figure out how to heal my soul. Somewhere along the path, I discovered that we are deeply connected, you and I. And that in order to heal myself, I must first heal my relationship with you.

I will write you a long letter, Mama. Together we will confront and unpack our lives together, and my life after you crossed over to the other side. Through this letter, I hope we will find our way back to each other's hearts. I hope my memories of you will become less painful, and that even though you have been gone for decades, we will reach a deeper understanding of each other as two women, connected by the strong bonds of having lived in the same body for nine months, and yet deeply disconnected on so many levels.

My letter to you comes from a place of love, and from wanting only to understand, and be understood. I only seek to connect with you, and with myself, so that I can learn to remember my own value in this world. I expect that the process will be difficult, but I also expect that it will be worth it for us both, and for many others with stories similar to ours.

The Child Within

Mama, I had my first ever therapy session a few years ago. I have made a lot of attempts at self healing over the years, but this was the first time I actually went to a trained therapist to try and figure myself out. The session was intense. I ended up crying like a child. Mama, anyone who knows me will tell you that I don't cry. My tears are stubborn, and more often than not, they fall backwards into my soul.

Turns out, my perception of my own life was very much connected to my perception of your life, and I felt unworthy of the many successes that I have had in my life, both professionally and personally. Deep down, I've often felt like I don't belong anywhere, and everyday I expect that somebody will show up and expose me for occupying spaces that do not belong to me. I expect that people will leave me, and things will be taken away from me. And so I hide, self-efface, apologize for my existence, and get out of the way for more deserving people to grab opportunities presented to me.

I want to tell you about something that came up during this session. It was a Rapid Transformational Therapy session, with hypnosis being a major part of it (I know, hypnosis is a little way out there for us, but I have changed a lot over the years, and definitely become more open-minded to different ways of doing life). Under hypnosis, I went back to a time when I was around four years old. Somehow, I was four again, and I was sitting on the cold, concrete floor in our old house. The therapist asked how I felt. I said I was okay, but that my mother was very sad, and angry. My father was absent.

Nothing out of the ordinary happened in that scene. It was more the feelings I was experiencing in that moment. I sat there looking out into the world, feeling alone, scared, confused, helpless. I felt all these things, but I also sensed a shield around me, and it felt like acceptance, like knowing that things were not right, but accepting them for what they were.

Hypnosis was nothing like I had imagined it would be. I was fully aware of myself and what I was saying. It was almost like an out of body experience. I knew and could feel that I was a thirty something year old woman, but I was also able, at the same time, to be a four year old girl, and even speak as softly as though I were four years old. I could feel the feelings of my younger self and articulate those feelings to the therapist.

We stayed in that scene with my four-year-old self for a little while. Asked how I felt about my father, I could not come up with anything to describe my relationship with my father. Instead, I said that I had to be loyal to my mother. I realized that my feelings about my father at that age hinged on what I believed you wanted them to be. He was mostly absent from our lives, and I don't believe I had formed a real opinion about him yet.

We visited two other scenes in my childhood, both of which were instances where I felt unsafe, scared, confused, or guilty. I will tell you more about the other scenes when we get to them. The therapist said my mind took me to those scenes because they were examples of what led to my developing the kind of self defeating beliefs that I had; the kinds that stood in the way of my ability to fully embrace the power and brilliance within me.

Mama, I am choosing to write this letter to you, not because you did anything wrong, but because my early experiences with you played a major role in the person that I became. My father did a lot of things that impacted me as well, but when I think of him now, I think of him as someone that was my biological parent, but with whom I never got to develop much of an emotional connection. What I feel for my father is mostly anger, whereas what I feel for you is a deep longing for connection. I am taking this step towards you because I realize now that I cannot live a fully productive life without healing the parts of me that are still stuck on the events of my childhood.

Earning the Light

Mama, the stories I heard about my grandmother elicited both fear and admiration. She was a larger than life presence that was mysterious, yet present and loving. She would sweep me up in suffocating hugs, kiss my face, tell me that she loved me, shower me with praise, call me by the pet name *Korera* (a special name that mothers of a married couple use to refer to each other) owing to the fact that I was named after your mother, but I could never truly accept her affection. For one thing, it was painfully awkward, because open displays of affection were not part of what was considered normal in our household. We did not hug each other, let alone kiss and smother each other with loving words. It almost felt wrong.

My grandmother's affection did not feel true, mostly because I had heard you tell stories about how much she disliked you. I could not accept the affection of a woman that disliked my mother. I didn't realize it then, but I was desperate for your approval, and your affection. I was like a desperate puppy, always seeking you out, even when you clearly did not have the energy or the desire to give me what I needed from you.

Mama, I wish I met you before your marriage to my father broke you. You were so beautiful. I look at your pictures as a young woman, gorgeous and alive, and I wonder where that woman disappeared to. The woman that was so beloved, the teacher, the adoring sister that served her siblings so selflessly, the sister-in-law and friend that is still so fondly remembered decades after her passing, and that got so many children named after her.

Your sisters have the most amazing stories about growing up with you. You were hardworking, industrious, and always ready to do whatever needed to be done to help the family. You happily picked up any slack at home and made sure everyone was okay. You were a happy young woman, much beloved by your family and the community around you.

I wonder how your life would have turned out had you married someone other than my father. Maybe you would still be alive today. Maybe you would never have had to go through the hell that you went through that ultimately led to your early death. More times than I can count, I wished I had a different father. I loved my father, but I wanted you to have married someone that didn't make you so sad. If I had to give my father up for you, I would have done it in a heartbeat.

While your side of the family was simple, down to earth, and full of love for you, my father's family was shroud in mystery and frequent outbursts of drama. His mother was this grand presence of a matriarch that I secretly resented and mildly feared. Everything about my grandmother's physical appearance suggested that she was a nice, loving, and kind old woman. But the stories we heard about her painted a different picture. I was wary of her affection. Like my father, she was a presence in my life that seemed harmless and loving on the outside, but that I knew had some darker layers inside.

Looking at my grandmother was like looking at the older, female version of my father. She was very fond of her son, and hearing her speak about him, you would think my father was one of the best things that ever graced God's good earth. She had ten children, but it was quite evident which of the ten were her favorite. My father was top of that list. In addition to looking like a replica of her (the soot dark complexion, the bright white teeth, and the delicately fine facial features), he had made a success of his life financially, and that brought a lot of honor to their family back in the village. Naturally, his mother took a lot of pride in her son's success.

Mama, we lost my grandmother recently, almost thirty years after your passing. She lived a full life, and maintained her strength and dignity to her very last breath. When news of her passing reached me, I took a small step back to reflect on her life, and acknowledge that it was the end of an era for our family. I helped write her eulogy, and in that process of recounting her life, I thought a lot about the woman that she was. She knew all her grandchildren by name, and even some of her great grandchildren. She never forgot who I was, even when she was at the end of her life and could barely walk. Whatever else she may have done in her life, right or wrong, she was indeed the last piece of duct tape holding the larger family together.

Mama, the last time I saw her, my grandmother called me a Light. She named three people in our extended family that she considered to be a Light, and I was one of them. A few years prior, as she saw me off to the airport, she had told me about an uncle that, in her view, was a Light in the family. She said this uncle was anointed as a child, taken in by the Catholic Church, and that he had grown to be a blessing and a Light to the entire family. She said that I had an opportunity too, and that I should make the most of it. She blessed my path as I got ready to start a new chapter of my life in the United States of America. To be honest, Mama, I didn't think anything of what my grandmother was telling me at the time. In fact, I almost never thought about her the entire time I was abroad. It wasn't until I was much older that I realized the value of what she told me that day. Her words started to make sense when I embarked on my journey of self-discovery. When I visited her in the months leading up to her death, and she finally included me in her list of family "Lights", I wanted to fall at her feet and cry. Not only because she affirmed my Light, but also because I felt terribly empty and she was the last shred of family roots that I had to hang on to.

My grandmother was nearing the end of her life. I felt closer to her then than I ever had before. I was at a point in my life where I was looking for identity, for some roots to anchor myself on. I felt that she was the closest I could come to having a parent again, and I was trying hard to hold on to her even as her body gave way to old age. I was eager to take as many pictures with her as possible, but she didn't have the patience for that. She curbed my enthusiasm and firmly told me that she wanted to spend time talking to me, not taking pictures.

Mama, I am ashamed to say that I listened very carefully to what my grandmother was telling me that day, but I did not understand half of it. Language was a major barrier. I never learned Kisii beyond the basics that I gleaned from you. Nobody else ever spoke Kisii to me, and over the years, even the little I already knew started to fade away. What I remember though is that my grandmother told me that I am a Light, and that as she comes to the end of her life, she is leaving her essence in me.

I struggled with my grandmother's death. She maintained her love for me, even though I had mistrusted and rejected her my entire life so far. I had listened to the stories people told about her, and although what I actually saw her do most of the time was pray earnestly and work at keeping the family together, I believed the dark tales. When we were younger, sometimes we would wake up with cuts on our bodies, and the joke would be that our grandmother had used some kind of magic to send sharp razor blades flying through the night to cut us. It was supposed to be funny, but I somewhat believed it. The cuts could have been from anything, considering we lived in such deplorable conditions, but it was easier to blame them on a known enemy than to actually face the fact that our home was a pathetic mess.

In the years after your passing, our grandmother would visit and bring us farm produce, but we would never eat any of it. At the time, we did not trust her at all. Everything she brought, we gave away to neighbors, or threw out when she wasn't looking. I believed my entire childhood that my grandmother was actively trying to harm us. Her tumultuous relationship with you had ingrained in me the notion that she was not and could never be an ally. My opinion of my father was no different. I adored him, but was deeply convinced that under the right circumstances, he could actually kill me.

The Missing Keys

Mama, I have written many times about your near death experience at the hands of my father. When I was in high school, I wrote about the events of that night all the time. It was like a clog in my psyche that I was desperately trying to clear in order to be able to move forward. I was never able to unclog myself of the trauma. I shared my writing with classmates and other girls. I'm not sure what I was looking for from them, but I never quite got what I needed. Maybe I needed them to tell me that it was okay to still be thinking about it so many years later, that it was okay to be stuck on it, and that it was also okay to let it go if I could. Maybe I was looking for some kind of acknowledgement, and validation. I'll never know, but what I knew was that the memory of that night kept replaying in my mind, and I felt that I needed to put it down on paper over and over again. When asked, I would vehemently deny that the story was real. I tried to pass it off as fiction, but everyone knew there was something about it that was deeply personal.

I was three or four years old. This is one of the earliest memories I have of my life. My brothers, Nicco and Austin, and I were sitting at the dining table quietly having our dinner. My father was in your bedroom. He kept calling out for you. Every time he called, you jumped and rushed over to the bedroom. He was yelling at you, and you were running up and down the house desperately looking for something (I later learned you were looking for my father's missing keys). At the same time, you were trying to help my little brother, Austin, eat his dinner. I remember you making several frantic trips back and forth between your bedroom and the dining room; looking for the missing keys, feeding your little toddler, and responding to my father. My father's voice got angrier and angrier every time he yelled out for you.

I sensed the tension in the house. My heart raced in my chest. I did not understand what was happening, but clearly something was wrong. I sat quietly and kept eating my dinner.

You went into your bedroom again, and suddenly we heard a loud scream. My brothers and I jumped up from the dining table and ran into our room. We closed the door behind us and sat huddled on the cold floor next to the wall. Your cries and screams pierced the night, like the cries of a lone victim dying alone in the cold wilderness, while everyone else curled up in their relative safety, pretending not to hear her. Not a single neighbor showed up to help. You screamed and screamed, and the entire estate of about sixteen households remained silent behind their closed doors.

"Inki okombori?" you cried. You asked my father the same question over and over again. "What are you asking me?"

I could hear furniture being thrown around. There were some stools in your room, and my father was using those, and anything else he could find, to hit you. With every thud your screams got weaker. Until finally there was nothing. I couldn't hear you anymore.

There was a long silence. Not a sound.

I felt death in the house. My chest was so tight I thought I would die. I was certain my father had killed you. And that he was coming for us next.

A little sound came through the air. Some movement. My heart jumped and started to pound so hard I was afraid he could hear the sound. I was not ready to die. My brothers sat quietly beside me.

I heard my father drag something across the floor and into the living room. Then silence.

"Mami!" he yelled. I jumped. Everyone called me Mami well into my teenage years (because you named me after your mother and called me Mami).

He yelled out my brothers' names as well. We quickly opened our bedroom door and rushed to the living room.

You were lying on the cold cement floor. Your thin, permed hair was scattered haphazardly on your swollen and bloody face. Your dress was ripped halfway down the front, revealing pale, prematurely wrinkled skin. You looked dead. There was a thin streak of blood coming out of your mouth, and more throughout your face and clothes.

We stood a safe distance away. My father yelled for us to move closer. He told us to stand next to what seemed like your lifeless body.

"Look at your mother," he said. "Look at her really well, because this is the last time you are going to see her alive."

We stood next to you and looked at you. Mama, it's been almost three decades since that night. The image of my father towering over your unconscious, blood-covered body haunts me to this day.

We stood there for what seemed like a long time. My father sat down on a sofa and lit a cigarette. He smoked it slowly, casually, as he watched us cowering next to your unconscious body.

Mama, sometimes I ask myself what could possibly have been wrong with my father to make him do what he did to you that night. I've asked myself that question many times over the years, but no explanation I have been able to come up with has made any sense. Maybe he was going through something, or he resented you for something, or maybe that is just who he was. Maybe he'd endured his own share of trauma as a child, or as an adult, or maybe he'd been socialized to believe the only way he could prove his masculinity and dominance over women was through violence. None of that explains the amount of brutality that went into what I witnessed that night. Was my father just plain evil?

"You better take a very good look because I am going to kill her tonight," he said.

Eventually, my father sent us back to our room. We went into our bedroom and closed the door.

I heard him drag you back into your bedroom. There was a long silence. I could picture my father smoking over your seemingly lifeless body. He was probably waiting for you to wake up so that you could witness him killing you. He probably wanted you to feel the pain, to scream for mercy, to feel the life slipping through the grasp of your weakened hand.

My brothers and I sat on the floor in silence. I did not have the slightest idea what was going through their minds, but at that young age, I had very little understanding of the fact that we were going through a shared life-altering experience. Three decades later, I have never had a single conversation with my brothers about that night. I have never heard them mention it, or any of the other traumatic things that we witnessed in those early years of our lives. It is as though we each made an unspoken decision to experience our childhoods together, but process everything individually without ever speaking to each other about it.

Suddenly, like a bolt of lightning cutting through the night sky, I heard scrambling, and a flash of movement. Someone made a horribly painful sound, zoomed out of the house, and banged the door behind them. I sat very still, waiting for a reaction from my father. I didn't see you run out of the house, but somehow I knew it was you. I knew you had escaped, and I felt a great sense of relief that you were not dead.

My father paced up and down around the house for a while. I could sense his upset. I expected he would burst into our room and take his anger out on us.

Surprisingly, my father did not try to follow you after you escaped. From the smell of cigarette smoke that lingered in the air throughout the night, I could tell that he smoked a good number of cigarettes that night. He did not come into our room either. The house remained eerily quiet, engulfed in the weight of my own fear and my father's cigarette smoke.

I fell asleep on the cold floor. In the morning, my father woke us up, gave us breakfast, prepared my older brother and I for school, and sent us on our way. I remember him being very warm and gentle with us in the morning. There was no mention of what had happened the previous night. He dressed me up neatly in my nursery school uniform, helped me put on my socks and my shoes, and even had me sit on his lap. At that moment, I was not afraid of him anymore. He was my father again. I sat on his lap and my heart did not jump for fear that he might kill me. It was almost as though the previous night had never happened.

When we came back from school that afternoon, you were back home. You had my little brother, Austin, strapped on your back as you went about your household chores. Your eyes were swollen to the point of being almost shut. You had deep bruises all over your body, which became permanent scars that you carried for the rest of your life.

None of us said anything about what happened. I pretended not to see your wounds, and you pretended they did not exist. My father sat comfortably on his favorite sofa, like royalty, and smoked unbelievable amounts of cigarettes while you ran up and down desperately trying to keep your marriage and your home afloat.

For many nights after that, I feared it was going to happen again. I feared that my father would wake up in the middle of the night and kill us all. Everybody else seemed to have forgotten about the incident and was going about their lives like nothing had happened, but I remembered every detail of it. I lost sleep worrying about something terrible happening. Any movement at night jolted me and triggered feelings of panic. Mama, that must have been my first real encounter with anxiety, and the genesis of many fears, real and imagined, that I carried for years throughout my childhood and young adulthood.

My father remained unapologetic. He carried on like a king, sitting back and having you serve him all day long whenever he was around. I heard that you slept outside in the bushes after your great escape that night. You slept on the cold, wet ground, without a sweater or blanket, covered only by your own blood and whatever was left of your tattered clothes. The area was full of mosquitoes, snakes, and God knows what other creatures. Sometimes I picture you coiled up in those bushes, cold, swollen from the assault and from the mosquito bites, barely alive, oblivious to the dangerous creatures crawling around, and afraid only for your children. And on the other hand, I see my father sitting on his throne of a chair, legs spread in carefree arrogance, oozing power as he smokes his third packet of cigarettes for the day. Mama, how can I not hate my father's guts?

In the months, and maybe years that followed, I temporarily forgot the events of that night. I was only occasionally reminded when I heard you talk to my older sisters, who were in boarding school when it happened, about how my father had tried to kill you. You carried numerous scars from that night as permanent reminders. My father had assaulted you with stools and other furniture, and the scars reflected the enormous extent of damage they had caused.

Mama, witnessing that night did something to my soul. I learned deep fear, and I also learned fierce protection of self. Over the years, I swore to myself that I would never let any human being do to me what I saw my father do to you. And so I learned to react very strongly to any threats of violence. My childhood fights with my brothers became fierce. For some reason, fighting was a normal part of our day to day interactions. You did not seem bothered when we threw punches and fought each other like animals. I had lots of pent up anger, and I held none of it back when someone tried to fight me. I wasn't necessarily strong physically, but the rage inside me was scary enough to give me an edge.

Years later, after the childhood fights had long stopped, my older brother, Nicco, woke up one morning and physically assaulted me. I was nineteen years old. As I lay on the ground, too shocked to scream, I had flashbacks of your near death experience in the hands of my father. Mama, I am sorry to say that even though he apologized over and over again, I have never been able to forgive my brother. I completely shut him out of my life. My guess is that he has become a symbol of abuse in my life. Every time I think about forgiving him, I experience the shame and pain of being at the mercy of a man all over again. Physical abuse has become a major trigger for me, and one of my biggest relationship deal breakers.

The Super Child

Mama, I have very few memories of you being happy. I remember one time you got up and did a dance for us. It was very basic. You had on your headscarf, as you always did, and a *lesso* tied around your waist. The memory of you getting up and making those little moves around the room, gently shaking your shoulders, nodding your head, with a big smile on your face, is vividly etched in my mind. I cherish that memory. You had your moments when you pulled a song from your past and poured your heart into the lyrics. Two of those songs still echo in my mind when I think of you. One was a gospel song about the passion of Christ, and the other an old song about a Kisii prophet that warned the community against resisting British colonization due to the great mayhem that the British were capable of unleashing on the people.

I also remember one afternoon when my older sisters came home from boarding school. It was an ordinary day, with the same old heat scorching our faces and the same old silence engulfing the air. I was somewhere minding my own business when I heard that my sisters were home. You were beside yourself with joy. It was as though the day suddenly changed and everything became brighter and happier, and noisier. The girls were beautiful. Their faces shone, and they carried that majestic aura of boarding school. I was in such awe of my sisters, even though there was always a strange divide between myself and them. To be fair, there was a strange divide between myself and everyone around me, probably because I was quite withdrawn. I observed and absorbed the world around me way more than I actively participated in it.

That evening, you told us that a neighbor had made a comment that she didn't realize you had such beautiful and "super" children. I remember you being ecstatic about it, and very proud that the neighbor had affirmed the beauty and value of your older children. You spoke at length, especially about my sister Bonareri, marveling at how beautiful she was. It was quite obvious that she was your favorite child. Oftentimes, you told her, and us, that she would win beauty pageants and become Miss Kenya.

I did not disagree with you. My sister was beautiful. She had perfectly shaped facial features, and a happy, bubbly personality, which accentuated her beauty. I had a lot of admiration for both of my older sisters. They were in boarding school and they knew a lot of things beyond our little, quiet town. It helped too that they made you happy. Whenever my sisters were around, somehow you were less angry, less tired, and less likely to beat us up for every little mistake that we made.

I never saw you beat my sisters. My brothers and I got the brunt of your anger almost on a daily basis. My sisters were older, and they probably needed a different kind of discipline than we did. But at the time, it felt as though they were special.

Mama, my sister Lena and I have spent a lot of time talking about our experiences of you, and especially of your anger. Understandably, Lena and I experienced you very differently, and our struggles as a result of having been raised by you are far from the same. While I got the sick and depressed version of you, Lena and Bonareri got the younger, happier, and healthier version of you. Lena struggles with her own memories of you, but in a more protective way. She knew you longer than I did, has more stories of you, and sees her life with you as having been fairly normal. I, on the other hand, feel deeply empty and desperate for your love and acceptance, which I craved but could not seem to get in your lifetime.

Lena and Bonareri spent their early years living with you and my father's side of the family at his rural home in Kisii. My father had built a small mud-walled house with an iron sheet roof near my grandmother's little place. Not many people in the area could afford iron sheet roofs, and so my father's house was quite respectable at the time.

Lena was a bit of a head-strong child, and she got in trouble a lot. She was tall, thin, with skinny legs and a triangular shaped chin. Her complexion was slightly darker than Bonaneri's, and a few shades darker than mine. I was born with the lightest complexion in our family. Lena took risks, was bold, and though not in any way outspoken, she knew how to stand her ground. Bonareri was shorter in height, had a rounder face, and looked less skinny because of her shorter frame. She was often told that she had a face like that of an Asian. She is also the one that looked the most like you amongst all the siblings; the round face, the eyes, the body frame. She was like a younger version of you. And you held her close to your heart.

Physically, what I got from you was mostly the skin complexion. While my father was soot dark, your skin had a light caramel tone to it. I took after you, and was in fact a few shades lighter than you. As a child I was tall and skinny. The height did not carry into my adulthood, but while it lasted, I was projected to potentially take after my father's sisters, all of whom were tall, towering women. The shape of my face was more straight, somewhere in between Lena's triangular face and Bonareri's round face.

Our personalities were as different as our faces. Lena was head-strong and action oriented. Bonareri was a social butterfly, and had quite a mouth on her. Quarelling with her was a losing battle. She could beat someone to the ground with her words alone. I was a quiet but fiery child. For the most part, I was invisible. I stayed out of people's way. I had a lot of fear and avoided conflict as much as possible. But when any of my siblings brought a fight to me, I would gladly engage. I fought hard, especially with my brothers. Being a girl was never a factor when we fought as children as I was very capable of holding my own.

Although we fought often, my relationship with my brothers was fairly normal. We avoided each other at school, and at home, we only played together when other children were not around. Outside the family home, they tended to only play with boys while I hung around girls.

My sisters were a whole other story. I don't remember ever playing with my sisters. They were older, and they spent most of their time in boarding school. I did not find out until years after both you and my father were dead that my two sisters were in fact my half sisters. My father became their father when he married you. Mama, I admire that you never told us this. And I'm even more impressed that my father never mentioned it. The first time I heard this story was at my father's funeral. One of his sisters mentioned it in conversation with another woman. I was in the room minding my own business but could hear what they were saying. They were speaking in Kisii, a language I was not very fluent in, so when I heard that story, I convinced myself that I had not understood it well. I casually dismissed the story and never said anything about it to anyone. I heard the same thing mentioned again a few months later, and this time I could not talk myself into thinking I had heard it wrong a second time. Still I said nothing until years later when I heard the story straight from Lena's mouth.

I came to learn that in fact, not even Bonareri knew about it. She came to find out about her own paternity later in life. Even I heard about it before she did. Mama, I find it highly impressive that as far as any of us know, my father never did or said anything to suggest that my two sisters were any less of his children than the rest of us. Because my sisters' paternity was never an issue while you and my father were alive, it continued to be a non-issue for us.

One of my aunts recently shared a theory about the reason you treated us differently. She said that you loved my sister Bonareri more because her father was the love of your life. You were supposed to have married Bonareri's father, but when you were pregnant with his child, you found out that he was seeing another woman. The anger and hurt from that sent you right into marrying my father, even though you had rejected him for many years prior. Mama, your sister told me stories about how desperately my father pursued you. He was friends with your brother, and he started chasing you when you were fairly young. According to your sister, your mother despised my father as a potential partner for you because of his dark complexion. She told you and your sisters that she did not want you to bring any men with skin that dark to her house. But with two children, both of whose fathers were not in the picture, you decided to finally accept this man that seemed to be so deeply in love with you.

Mama, I am sorry that my father turned out to be your downfall. I am sorry that he did not treat you with the love, respect, and care that you deserved.

I don't know much about Lena's father, but I imagine your story with him did not go that well either. Lena once told me that she found out her father got you pregnant when you had just started nursing school. You were young, and ready to start on a path that would give you a great career as a nurse. Your mother was so proud of you, and she was looking forward to the happy and successful life that you would have. But the pregnancy forced you to drop out of college, thus killing your dream of becoming a nurse. After giving birth to my sister, you picked yourself back up and became an untrained teacher at a local school. You gained your dignity back, and through your hard work, and the goodness of your heart, you built many positive relationships, gaining the love and respect of your community. You had a good life again, until you married my father, left your teaching job, moved to a new town, and became a housewife. Your life went downhill from there.

Mama, maybe your story with my father was the reason you could not love me the same way that you loved my sister. Even as I say this, I am not entirely sure that it is fair. Maybe you did love me. Maybe you just did not know how to express that love. Recently, Lena and I had a conversation about this, and she said she once confronted you about not loving her. That was the way that she perceived your treatment of her at the time. Lena said that you were surprised when she told you this, and that you cried because to you, it was baffling that she would think that. Mama, I feel like that same conversation Lena had with you back then is the same conversation I am having with you right now.

Sometimes I feel like it is selfish and vain of me to be pining after your love so many years after your passing. Deep down, I know that you did love me like any mother would love her child. What confuses me though is that while you were mostly cruel to me, you expressed love in much healthier ways to Bonareri - your super child.

When my sister Bonareri was in upper primary, she transferred to the same day school that I was in. One day, we had a magician come to the school. The school was within a few short meters of our home, and so Bonareri asked me to run back home and ask you for two shillings to pay for the magic show. I was excited because I knew you would give us the money if I said Bonareri had asked for it. Had she not sent me, I would never have dared to show my face at home with the intention of asking for money.

I ran all the way home to get Bonareri two shillings for the magic show. You were sitting outside on a neatly woven mat, spread out under the shade of a tree. The line of one-bedroomed houses behind you looked beautiful in their maroon concrete splendor. Our family lived in the first two houses, which had been combined by taking down the wall between them to make a two-bedroomed house, while the rest of the houses were rented out to various families, many of whom were teachers at my school.

I coyly sat down next to you and repeated Bonareri's request. You immediately gave me two shillings for my sister, no questions asked. I hesitated for a moment, then proceeded to ask you if I could also have two shillings for the magic show.

Mama, I have never forgotten your anger when I asked for the two shillings for myself. You looked at me with rage and disappointment, and told me how selfish and ungrateful I was to even ask you for money when I knew well enough that you did not have money.

My heart was crushed. I went back to school, gave the two shillings to Bonareri, and looked for other things to occupy my time as other children, including my sister, went to see the magic show.

Another Woman's Child

Mama, it pains me to write about you like this. As a grown woman, I empathize with your pain. I know that you were hurting. But it is still a struggle to face my memories of you with objectivity, and without the natural filters that I would have as your child, as someone that is forever connected to you and that will love you till kingdom come, no matter what.

Do you remember Tano, Mama? Do you remember that young girl that came to live with our family, and that spent over five years working for us, raising your children?

I imagine Tano must have been a young teenager when she came to live with us, and closer to eighteen or nineteen when she left. It was common for families to have a live-in housegirl, many of whom, especially in the early 90s, were children. Sometimes they were relatives from less fortunate backgrounds. But Tano was from Tanzania, and her mother had handed her over to our family so she could work to support her family back home.

She was tall and slender, with a small, beautiful chocolate face that seemed hardened by a life of hardship. She did not usually chat much with us kids, but every now and then she told us stories about her family, and her community. Mama, I regret to admit that we were not very kind to her. Sometimes my brothers and I took the stories that she told us and made up songs to make fun of her. She was a good sport about it. Tano never raised her voice at us or treated us unkindly in any way. I saw her as quite passive, almost as though she did not have much agency in her own life.

Tano might certainly have wanted to take her anger out on us, but she could not. While you beat us as though we were not your own, you would never allow Tano (or even our big sisters) to hit us for any reason. The girl was terrified of you. She got just as much, if not more, beatings from you as we did. The difference was that Tano was grown. We were kids. She was older than Lena and Bonareri, but she got beaten even though Lena and Bonareri did not.

The beatings Tano received were often scary and shocking to me. I remember one time you accused her of washing the green vegetables she was about to cook in water that had her period blood in it. I didn't at that point know what period blood was. But I could see from your reaction that it was something very bad. Tano came from a community in Tanzania that, from what I heard, practiced witchcraft. It was not clear to me if putting period blood in food was meant to be a form of witchcraft, or if it was Tano's way of protesting the harsh treatment that she received from you. Having had her in our household for as long as I could remember, I did not see Tano as someone that would try to bewitch us. Not that I had the mind to think much of the situation at the time, but I was more inclined to think it was revenge.

Mama, you beat Tano so badly that day, I was afraid you would never stop. Then you called in the watchman, our security guard Etyang, to come and beat her some more.

Etyang was an interesting old man. Like most other people from the local Teso community, he had very dark skin. He was old but had a young and athletic looking form, which he covered with an oversized coat that was his signature attire whenever he came in for work. I'd known him for as long as I could remember, and he was the only person I knew that I could say was truly your friend. He came to our house every evening and told us all kinds of stories, both real and imagined. He also chain smoked cigarettes almost as much as my father did. I found that quite endearing, and it made him all the more appealing to me as a person, because the smell of cigarettes that he carried about him reminded me of my father. I remember Etyang telling us that cigarettes were rich in vitamin D. I believed him. He was like an extension of our family. Sometimes when you did not have money, and my father didn't send any, Etyang would go months without getting paid. But he still showed up for work every day, with the same drive and the same enthusiasm that he brought to his work no matter what else was happening in his life.

On the day that Tano washed the vegetables with her period blood, you called Etyang for back up. Etyang made Tano strip down to her underwear. He then took a large piece of cloth, dipped it in salty water and lay it on top of her almost naked body. He got a fat stick, and with it beat that poor girl, with the salty piece of wet cloth on top of her, until she bled. The point of him using the salty piece of cloth was so that when her skin broke, the salt would penetrate her wounds and intensify the pain.

Mama, the suffering Tano went through while in your hands haunts me to this day. Every time you beat her, I was terrified, but I also trusted that she deserved it. I trusted that you knew what you were doing, and that it was right. I remember the day her mother came for her. She said Tano was now old enough to get married, and that she was ready to be married off. Tano's opinion was not relevant in that decision. She did not seem happy or sad about going back home to get married. She accepted and went along with it, packed her little bag like a good girl, and followed her mother to the new life that awaited her in Tanzania.

Mama, I wonder if Tano ever got to make any decisions for herself, about her own life. Or if she moved from your hands, back to her mother's hands, and into the hands of a husband she did not get to choose.

Sometimes I wonder if what you did to Tano could have contributed to the suffering we have undergone as a family. She was a child, Mama. Another woman's child. And no matter what she did, she never deserved the beatings and humiliation that she endured at your hands. She did not deserve to have a man strip her naked and beat her through a salty piece of cloth until she bled.

We, your children, did not deserve to see that.

What's That Smell?

I was very quiet as a child. I remember feeling a lot of shame. Our family was relatively wealthy, compared to other families around us. In fact, we were the only family I knew that owned a car. And not just one car, but two cars, and two lorries. When I say, we owned these vehicles, I actually mean that my father owned the vehicles. We saw one or two of them maybe once a year when he came home for Christmas. We also owned three rows of rental houses and shops in Busia. Our family lived in two combined units, and we had about fourteen others rented out. We also had a shop that was rented out, and a posho mill that you managed sometimes. Other times one or the other of your relatives that came to visit us would run it.

Although we looked wealthy from the outside, we had very little. Sometimes our tenants went months without paying rent, my father did not show up or communicate for months, and you were probably too sick and depressed to manage the property.

I saw and felt your sadness very deeply. I carried it in my heart. It silenced me. When other children at school told me how lucky I was to be so clever at school and to come from a rich family, I smiled and remained silent. It was confusing to them why I would come to school in the same dirty and worn out uniform, sometimes without shoes, when my family was so wealthy. I understood that my father was wealthy, and I didn't necessarily think of you as being poor either, but I didn't experience wealth in my day to day life. In fact, the children that thought we were rich seemed to have more than I did. Many of them had at least some coins to buy a snack during snack break. Mama, I would never have dared ask you for money for a snack. Some children that didn't have money either would wait near the fence where local women sold snacks to school children, and they would follow the children with money to beg for tiny pieces of whatever snack they bought. I didn't have money, but I never begged anyone for their snack. I was too closed in for that. I accepted my situation for what it was and tried not to desire things I did not have.

Poverty seemed normal to me. I did not pity the kids who were worse off than we were because we all behaved the same. When

I went to school without shoes, I stepped in the fuming, toxic waste and urine on the pit latrine floor, same as everybody else. When I did not have a piece of paper to wipe my ass, I used leaves, same as everybody else. We all scooped fresh cow dung with our bare hands and used it to line the walls and floors of our mud-walled classrooms. None of it seemed disgusting to me. It was the reality of our lives at the time, and I accepted it fully as it was the only life that I knew.

I smelled. I know I did because you told me so.

I remember the one pair of panties that I had. It was originally beige in color, but the bottom part of it had turned almost black due to being worn everyday without washing. One time, I went to the market with you and saw some panties on display. At that moment, they looked like the thing I wanted the most in the world. So I gathered some courage and asked if you could buy me one. Your reaction was immediate and hostile. Not that I expected any different. I already knew that money was a sour subject for you and it was sure to trigger your anger. I cowered and never asked again.

Bathing was not part of our daily, or even weekly routine. We did not have a routine. Once in a while, you would yell at me that I smelled. That was the only cue I had that it was time to bathe, and maybe wash my panties. I remember coming to sit next to you on the sofa one evening. Usually I would avoid you as much as possible, but somehow you seemed safe to be around on that particular day. My sisters were home and you were in a better than usual mood. But the moment I sat down, you violently pushed me away and told me I smelled disgusting.

Mama, I longed to be close to you. I wanted to sit next to you, hear you talk. You sat with my sisters sometimes and had conversations with them. I desired that. I understood that they were older, and came home from boarding school only for short periods of time. You probably also had more to talk to them about than you did with me. But I still wanted to be able to sit with you too and have a conversation that wasn't about reprimanding or insulting me.

I remember you pushing me away a lot, and calling me a bad dog. That was your favorite insult: *Esese embe eye. Chotororo ya mkebe*. I still don't know what the second part of that insult means. It sounded to me like it could have something to do with diarrhea in a can. To be fair, it was an insult you hurled at all of us, including my sisters, whenever you were upset.

There were also times when I felt a tingling of love from you. Like the time I accompanied an older neighbor girl to the market and came home late. We were not allowed to leave the general area of our estate without permission. I figured no one would know as long as I was back home before dark. Unfortunately for me, it rained heavily that day. The area used to get frequent hail storms. It was impossible to walk in that storm. The neighbor girl and I had to seek shelter at the front of one of the shops at the market. By the time we got back home that night, you were frantic and had been looking for me for hours.

I got the beating of my life that day. The kids in my neighborhood talked about that beating for a long time. But I understood it as love. Mama, when I think about that beating, I don't remember your anger, or how much it hurt. I remember that you were terribly worried about me. That was one of very few times I saw genuine love and concern about my wellbeing from you.

There was also the time my younger brother pushed me and my forehead hit the corner of a wall. I got a large, scary looking swelling on my forehead. You were just leaving the compound when the incident happened. You heard my screams but did not come back to check what had happened. When you came back home in the evening, I had a swelling the size of a fist on my face.

I saw you cry for me that day. You cried and yelled and lined everybody up for a beating. Everyone, with the exception of myself, that was home when that incident happened got a thorough beating for letting you leave the compound without telling you that I was hurt.

I felt special for not getting beaten that day. My swelling looked bad, and I took advantage to make myself seem sicker than I actually was.

Over the next few days you cried for me many times. A neighbor advised you to take me to a hospital in the next town since we did not have any big hospitals in Busia.

I remember getting into a crowded *matatu* with you, and sitting on your lap. It was a long drive. Because we were so squeezed in the *matatu*, by the time we got there, my leg was numb and I could not stand on it. You carried me on your back all the way to the hospital. I must have been six or seven years old at the time, so I was not a small girl. Mama, that remains one of my fondest memories of you to this day.

Christmas Tree

You could never get lost looking for our home. Wonder Tree Estate was about the only individual-owned compound I knew in the area that actually had a name. The estate did not have a gate, but when you made the turn from the main road, you walked about a hundred meters along a driveway lined by towering cypress trees. For me, it was like walking across a long stage, with dozens of eyes on you. Our front door was directly ahead.

Every time I came home from school and you were sitting on the front steps of the house, I shrank with every step forward. I took a mental scan of myself and wondered what you were going to beat me up for that day. Was I walking too fast, or too slow? Did I come home too early, or too late? Did I forget anything that morning? Was I seen anywhere that I wasn't supposed to be?

My gait was awkward, mainly because I expected to be scolded any second, but sometimes because of inflammation between my legs. I wet my bed sometimes. And I went days, maybe even weeks without bathing. That, coupled with wearing the same underwear everyday, created mayhem between my legs. Lucky for me, many children in my school came from extreme poverty, and they smelled just as badly as I did, if not worse.

Walking up that path without your piercing gaze was always a relief. When you were not on the front steps, I could take in the majestic beauty of the cypress, pull up a blade of grass and chew on it, walk slowly, pause if I wanted to.

I didn't realize cypress trees could be anything more than some beautiful trees that lined up driveways and stuff until a neighbor came to ask if they could have a branch to use as a Christmas tree. We were all confused. Turned out we were sitting on a gold mine with all the trees that we had. Of course we gave it to her for free. To our family, the idea of decorating a tree for Christmas was laughable.

We did have fairly elaborate Christmas parties though. That was the one time of year that we were almost sure our father would be home. I was terrified of my father. But there was also a sense of safety for me when he was around. You would never so much as raise your voice at us when he was home. If we did anything wrong, the most you could do was give us that familiar stink eye, which meant we would get it as soon as he left.

Having our father around for Christmas also meant we got new clothes, new shoes, and a vast array of food; *nyama choma*, *chapati*, *mandazi*, soda, sweets. For the two or three days a year that he was with us, he was my hero. Home felt different. The smell of cigarette smoke penetrated the furniture, and lingered there for days. I loved the smell of cigarette smoke. And the smell of his after shave in the morning. With him around, home was special.

I was very much aware though that my father was the source of much of your sadness. I once heard you talk to a neighbor woman about the *ndogo ndogo* women that my father spent his money on. I was not exactly sure why my father would hang out with and spend his money on these women. But I could see that it made you sad.

Mama, do you remember the day my father was trying to hit you again, in our presence? My brothers and I were outside playing. We saw you run out of the house, with our father running right behind you. Once outside, he stopped running after you. You stopped running too but kept a safe distance between the two of you. He said some words to you in Kisii. I do not remember what he said, maybe because I did not understand the language well. You remained silent. He started walking towards you, threatening to beat you up. You retreated. He took a couple more steps towards you. You turned around and ran away, around the corner and out of sight.

My father called out for my brothers and I to come to him. We reluctantly walked over and stood next to the side of his car.

"Your mother is very stupid," he said. "She doesn't like progress. Have you ever encountered someone that doesn't like to make progress in life? That is your mother."

My brothers and I said nothing.

He went on a long rant about how stupid you were, occasionally throwing in a question to confirm that we agreed with him. We kept our eyes fixed on the ground, avoiding eye contact. I did not know how to react to what he was saying. A neutral face was the only option I had. I could not show any indication that I agreed or disagreed with him. If I agreed, I would have hell to pay because my brothers would definitely report it to you. If I disagreed, I would probably still have hell to pay because although he had never laid a hand on me, I knew that my father's violence was much worse than yours. You, as my mother, could beat me all day long, but I knew for sure that you could never really hurt me. My father on the other hand, I could not be too sure. I understood that with him, all it took was one beating, and he could end me.

When he came to the end of his rant, my father asked if we wanted to go live with him in Kisumu. We remained silent and avoided eye contact.

"You can all come with me right now," he said. "Just go pack a bag, and get in the car."

He waited for us to move. We stayed put.

"Do you want to come with me?" He started to lose his patience.

There was no way I was going anywhere with my father. I adored him, but I also had a deep fear that he could kill me. I also understood that between you and my father, you were the one that truly cared about us. My father was gentle and nice to us, but he could not be a parent that was there every day. I remember a story about a time you and my younger brother went to his house in Kisumu. My brother did something wrong, and my father's response was to literally throw him down the stairs and then follow him down to give him a beating. You were able to run to my brother and put yourself between the two in order to protect your child. If he could hurl my little brother down the stairs, he could do the same to me too.

When none of us responded to my father's suggestion that we go with him, he clicked his tongue, called us stupid, and told us to get out of his sight. He got into his car and drove away.

You cried that afternoon, Mama. Long and hard. We stood around your bed, swearing over and over again that we did not even want to go with our father. We recounted to you everything that he said about you, then swore desperately that we did not agree with any of those things. You could not speak. You buried your face in the palms of your hands and sobbed louder and heavier than I had ever seen you sob before.

Who Wants My Mother Dead?

Mama, in my hypnotherapy session, my therapist had me going back to when I was little. My mind went to a scene from my childhood that I vividly remember, but that I never previously thought much of. I am still unclear as to why, of all the things that happened in my childhood, that scene came to mind.

You were sitting on the floor. A woman, a stranger, was sitting on the sofa behind you, her thighs on either side of you as she plaited your hair into neat cornrows. I was sitting on the sofa, next to this woman, watching her work. Her face was dark and smooth, not a single visible blemish. She had a scarf tied on her head. I wondered if her hair was long and beautiful like yours. My own hair had never had a chance to grow beyond a centimeter or two. You kept my hair shaved to the scalp, and as much as I desired long hair, I would never have dared open my mouth to ask you about letting it grow out. Every time you reached for the scissors, I obediently sat down and let you cut my hair similar to how you cut my brothers' hair.

The two of you made some small talk, followed by long stretches of silence as she worked expertly on your hair. I was painfully bored. My brothers were outside playing with other children. I wanted to go outside.

I knew you wanted me to stay in the house. Before the hair woman arrived, you'd told me that you did not know this woman well, and that she could steal strands of your hair for witchcraft.

You told me all this in Kisii, and while I got the general gist of what you said, I was still quite unsure about what exactly you meant.

As I sat there, willing the torture of having to sit there and watch this woman to end, I started to question whether I had heard you correctly. I mean, there was no way you could possibly expect me to sit there until this woman finished making your entire head of hair, was there? And who steals people's hair anyway? It did not make sense to me. So I decided that I had heard you wrong.

I got up to leave the room. As soon as I got to the door, you yelled in Kisii, "Mami, where are you going?"

I hesitated for a moment, and then said, "Outside."

You made a familiar gurgling sound in your throat. It meant that you were disappointed, and upset.

"What did I ask you to do?"

I made my way back to the sofa and quietly sat down. Clearly, I had heard and understood you correctly the first time. I could see that you were fuming. You let me sit for a minute, then suddenly changed your mind and yelled at me to get out. You spoke in Kisii so the woman wouldn't understand. You said if I wanted to go outside I should go outside, and that I might as well kill you myself if that is what I wanted to do.

I tried to stay. Obviously I did not want you to die, and I would probably not have tried to leave the room if I was sure I had understood your instructions correctly. I was not a disobedient child. Questioning your instructions was not something I would ever dream of doing, and I was deeply disappointed in myself for getting off that seat to try and go outside. So I sat still and hoped you would allow me to correct my mistake.

You yelled at me to get out.

Later you scolded me for not caring if someone stole your hair and used it to bewitch and kill you. I was devastated. You were already sick, but I started to see it as my fault. Maybe if I had stayed and watched, you wouldn't have continued to get sicker.

This scene played out very clearly in my hypnotherapy session. I felt shame, and guilt, for making a mistake that could have cost you your life. As an adult, sitting in the therapist's home, I understood that the guilt was baseless. Nothing I did that day contributed to your death. But I still felt your disappointment in me, and your anger.

You continued to get sicker, and weaker. You said someone was trying to kill you. Someone was bewitching you. I was wary of everyone. Every time someone came to our house, I watched them as closely as I could. We did not eat anything anyone offered us. We did not go to anyone's house. We took every precaution. And yet your health continued to deteriorate.

On days when you were particularly unwell, you asked me to sleep with you in your bed. When my sisters were home, all of us girls slept in your room. My sisters slept on the floor and I slept with you in your bed.

One afternoon, my sister Bonareri, my brothers, and I were sitting outside your window as you slept in your room. We heard you make a strange sound. Because you were sick, and you often made strange noises due to the fever and the pain you were in, I did not think much of it. You made the sound again, this time louder. Soon you were making a lot of desperate sounding noises, as though you were puking and gagging all at the same time. We all jumped up and ran into your room.

There was blood everywhere. You were toppled over on the floor, vomiting blood with large chunks of fleshy things in it.

"Get the doctor," you cried.

Bonareri started screaming. Neighbors rushed in, and in no time our house was filled with people. Bonareri, my brothers, and I all ran to the nearest clinic, leaving you with my sister Lena, and a house full of neighbors. I took off without any shoes. I was aware that something was very wrong, but my mind was blank and my eyes were dry. Bonareri cried as we ran on the murram road. My tears were nowhere to be seen. I did not know what I was doing. I ran because my mother said we should get a doctor, but also because I thought Bonareri knew what she was doing and the best thing for me to do was to follow her.

We did not know any doctors. But at a clinic that was about a kilometer away, there was a man that was maybe a nurse. He gave us injections and bitter pills whenever we were sick with Malaria, so everyone considered him a doctor even though it was common knowledge that he was really probably a nurse.

The doctor that was not really a doctor listened to our story and asked us to go back home. He said he was coming right over. He stood there, helpless, watching him focus keenly on something he was writing in a counterbook. He was tall, of medium build, and probably in his late twenties or early thirties. He was a kind man. We had been to the clinic many times because it was the only clinic in the area, and he knew who we were. We stood there quietly, humbly communicating that we wouldn't leave without him. So after a little dilly dallying, he got up and followed us. He passed by a shop and bought some milk, and maybe eggs. He then walked behind us all the way to our house.

Our house was still full of people when we got back home. The doctor went inside your room. I squeezed my way through the crowd and got into your room too. You were lying on the bed, your head propped up with pillows. The floor and your bed were full of blood. There was a bucket next to your bed. It also had some blood in it.

The doctor gave you some milk. You vomited again. A woman inside your room started to cry. Watching a grown up cry gave me anxiety, so I made my way out of the house.

About an hour later, an ambulance arrived at our house. You were carried into the back of it. Lena and the doctor went with you as they ferried you to a hospital in the next town, Bungoma.

Some neighbors came over and scooped all the blood into the bucket. They cleaned up your room, but left the blood in the bucket. That night, the doctor came back. He took some samples from the bucket of blood, including some of the fleshy chunks. It looked as though you had vomited chunks of your internal organs out.

Over the next few days, we continued to go to school as usual. I did not cry. I did not tell anyone at school what had happened to you. Somehow, it felt like a shameful thing. The teachers, and some students, knew about it because some of them lived in our compound. But nobody asked me anything, and I did not say anything. I went about my days as though nothing had happened.

You were admitted at the hospital, and so my father came to stay with us for a while. He brought in a witch doctor to cleanse our house. The man moved around the house chanting and rubbing ashes on various surfaces. My father said we needed to be protected too. One by one we were brought before the witch doctor. Using a sharp razor blade, he cut three short but deep lines on the back of each of our right hands. He then rubbed some ashy substance on the wounds and declared that we were now protected. No one would be able to look at us with bad eyes or bewitch us.

It seemed like a long time that you were at the hospital. One night, unexpectedly, my father showed up with you in the car. You were lying down on the reclined front passenger seat. You looked weak. But you were home.

I was elated. After you vomited blood, I remember hearing someone say you could not recover from that. That there was no way someone could vomit that much blood and survive. And so subconsciously I had started to prepare myself for the worst. Having you back home was both a relief and a great moment of proving people wrong. You arrived at night, but I couldn't help myself. I went around some neighbors' houses to let them know that you were back home.

The Sisters

My father left to go back to work a few days after you came home. You were back on your feet, but you were so weak you could barely walk more than a few steps at a time. Many afternoons you sat outside on a mat under the shade of a tree. I sat with you sometimes. In silence. You were kinder now. But you still had moments of unexpected angry outbursts.

The women in our estate were loud and sometimes obnoxious. They shouted at their children, gossiped about each other, and on occasion had open quarrels where difficult words and sentiments were expressed. You never participated in any of that. There were occasions when I thought you, as landlady, would intervene. But you never did. You stayed out of other people's quarrels.

One time two women got into a fight that escalated to a war of words in the presence of the whole estate. It was around seven o'clock in the evening, dark outside, but early enough that most families were still outside preparing dinner for their families. The estate had two rows of one-bedroom houses, with the exception of our house, which had combined two units to make a two-bedroom house. The houses were all connected to each other, each sharing a wall with the next house. On our row, there was a common veranda at the back that ran all the way across from the first house to the last.

Most families liked cooking right outside their doors on the shared veranda. On this night, two women were outside cooking when a quarrel erupted. The insults started small and grew as other women laughed and cheered them on. Some mothers sent their children inside, since some of the insults were too inappropriate for children. You seemed to be in your own world. You did not laugh, did not participate, did not send us inside. I still remember my little brother laughing hysterically as grown women hurled angry insults at each other.

There was also the tenant that brought home a different woman every time. He owned a motorbike, and dressed himself in flashy outfits that made him look like a celebrity. The neighbors gossiped about him a lot. Rumor had it that he had AIDS and was spreading it around. A few times we unknowingly picked up used condoms from around his house. We did not know what they were. Every time we saw him coming home with a woman, we ran to you to report that we saw him coming home with a *ndogo ndogo maringo saba*. The phrase in itself made no sense, but it was generally used by the neighbors to mean that the woman was young, attractive, and probably a prostitute.

I do not remember you stopping us from participating in these rumors even though you paid no attention to the rumors yourself. You were consumed by your own sorrow. Mostly silent, mostly sleeping, or moaning in pain. You had no friends. Except the old security guard, Etyang, who came to our house every evening. I suspect he came over mostly because he was assured of getting some dinner, but he was also a light in the darkness that engulfed our family.

Etyang told a lot of tall tales that were highly captivating, but often untrue. Most nights, as soon as he came from our house, he went to his usual spot outside, made himself comfortable, and fell deep asleep. One time, as he was sleeping, we went over and took his torch, coat, *panga*, and other things that he had around him. We hid them in the house and waited. The next morning Etyang came to our house, breathing heavily.

"You will never believe what happened," he said.

He then proceeded to narrate this great ordeal that he went through in the night. He said some thieves came to our estate and he spent most of the night fighting them off. He said there were so many of them but he fought really hard and injured some of them. Finally they took out a gun and he ran away, climbed a tree and spent the night up on the tree. The thieves then made away with his coat, torch, *panga*, and other things. We laughed and laughed, humored him for a while before giving him back his stuff. Despite evidence to the contrary, Etyang stuck by his story. He swore he really did spend the night fighting with thieves.

These moments of light, and the focus on other people's problems, provided respite for us at a time when you were fading away right in front of our eyes. I went to school and got stellar grades. Surprisingly, I was appointed class monitor. I barely ever talked to anyone at school, but for some reason, maybe because I aced my academics so effortlessly, the teacher decided that I was a good fit for that position.

Despite my silence, I was well liked at school. Some girls kept asking if they could come to my house. I always said no. I said my mother wouldn't allow me to have friends over. But the truth was that I did not want them to see you. I did not want them to feel the gloom that was in our house.

Mama, I remember the day your sisters came to see you. You were sitting outside on a mat when they appeared at the turn from the mainroad. You saw them immediately. Aunt Rebecca, her tall and slender frame looking majestic against the towering cypress trees on either side of the driveway. And Aunt Robina, shorter, chubbier, filled with so much life, and so much heart.

Aunt Robina had visited a number of times before. She seemed to be the closer one to you, of your two sisters. She was also the closer one to us since we knew her a little bit more. I had heard a lot about your family, but I do not think I had met your sister Rebecca before this visit.

The moment you saw your sisters, your floodgates opened and you started sobbing uncontrollably. You painfully gathered yourself from the mat and started making your way towards them. Your sisters also started wailing. They ran to you, and when you all met somewhere along the driveway, all three of you threw yourselves to the ground, in each other's arms and sobbed together.

I stared. I did not fully understand what was happening, why everyone was crying. I knew though that what I was witnessing was an expression of love. It was the tears, and the amount of pain that seemed to be behind it, that I did not fully understand. You spoke very fondly about your sisters. I almost envied them. Seeing you love someone so deeply, and so openly, was both beautiful and painful.

During the time your sisters were with us, the mood in our house changed. You seemed stronger, more alert. You talked more. All three of you cried a lot. But you were happier. Your sisters hugged me a lot, gave me lots of kisses, which were unfamiliar and slightly uncomfortable. They bought us treats and showered us with a lot of love. They were like an ocean of love, with overwhelming gushes that were almost suffocating. I had never in my life seen you behaving like that. It was confusing how your sisters could be like that when I can barely remember a time in my life when you gave me so much as a hug.

No Goodbyes

That year, my father did not come home for Christmas. We waited, spent days looking up the driveway, expecting that his car would appear along the turn any minute. It never did. You made no comments about his absence. At this point, you no longer talked about my father. That was the first Christmas I could remember that my father had failed to come home. There were no new clothes, no shoes, no treats, and definitely there was no Christmas party. We went to church, came back home, and spent the day like it was any other day in the year.

The silence in our lives was deafening. One day, a few days before my ninth birthday, I came home from school to find you gone. A neighbor told us you had gotten worse that morning, and my sister Lena had gone with you to Bungoma Hospital. The last time you went to Bungoma Hospital, you'd stayed there for weeks. I did not need to be told that you were not coming back home anytime soon.

The next day at school, some girls told me that their parents were talking about how sick you were when you were taken to hospital. Some well-wishers on the road helped you get transport. You could not walk.

I was ashamed that other children in school knew about what happened to you. I listened to their stories but said nothing. I did not cry or react in any way. I don't think I could. It was never that I put any effort into not crying or reacting. I simply couldn't.

A few days later, we had a sports day at school. I was hanging around the fence of the school when I saw a big lorry with the words Wonder Tree Ltd written boldly on its side. I knew instantly that that was my father's vehicle. I had never seen it before, but Wonder Tree Ltd was the name of my father's business. He owned an insurance brokers company and also had a handful of other businesses.

Being a sports day, the gates were open and we could walk in and out of school at will. So I ran out of school and followed the lorry. As I was running along the road, a similar lorry came from behind. Like the first one, it had the words Wonder Tree Ltd written on it. Our home was very close to the school. I saw the lorries making the turn towards our house and that confirmed that they were indeed my father's vehicles.

My father was already home when I got there. It was good to see him, especially after we'd missed him that Christmas. He was in good spirits. He told me to go get my brothers from school because we were moving. We were going to live with him in Kisumu.
"Where is Mama?" I asked.

He said you were at the hospital. But that you were fine. He said you might be at the hospital for a while, and so we had to go live with him.

The adrenalin of moving so suddenly from the only home I had ever known did not afford me time to overthink the situation. Under different circumstances, moving to my father's house would have been a scary idea. But we had been alone for days since my mother was taken to hospital, and so my father coming for us was a relief.

I ran back to school, walked around looking for my brothers, said goodbye to a few girls, and then went back home to pack. Our entire house had already been packed into the lorry by the time I got back home. The lorries left. We stayed behind with our father for a while as he talked with some neighbors to make arrangements for how the estate would continue to run in our family's absence. My mother had some goats, chicken, and a cow. They were left in the care of one of our tenants. We never saw them again.

When everything was wrapped up and my father was ready, we got into his car, drove down the cypress-lined driveway, and I said goodbye to our Busia home forever. As an adult, I have been there a few times since, but only as a visitor. I didn't realize when I ran home after my father's lorries that that would be the last time I stepped on that ground while it was still home. I didn't realize I would never walk up that driveway again and shrink under my mother's gaze as I made my way home. The permanence of that move did not hit me for a long time.

It was late evening when we got to the next town, Bungoma, where you were admitted. My father agreed to pass by the hospital briefly so we could see you.

You lay face up on the hospital bed. It was a private room, and my sister Lena was sitting on a chair next to your bed. I sat on the bed. You looked at us and smiled weakly. You did not say a word. We all just sat there quietly. My father asked Lena some questions about how you were doing. She answered. We sat with you in silence. My eyes were fixed on you. I wanted you to say something, to get up. Even your anger would have been better than the silence at that point. I could see that you were aware we were there, but all we got was a smile, and blank stares into the ceiling.

Soon it was time to go. We got up and followed our father out of the room. I do not remember saying goodbye. There were no hugs, no tears, no promises. We simply got up and walked away.

CHAPTER TWO

Dear Mama,

My father's house was a mansion indeed. Coming from Busia, where I did not know anyone that lived in a two-story house, to this large town where there were large mansions everywhere, and tarmacked roads with many twists and turns, was a dream. The first night we arrived at the house, my brothers and I ran from room to room, amazed at the sheer size and beauty of it. I had never been to my father's place. Of the three of us younger siblings, only my little brother had. My sisters and older brother on the other hand had been there many times before because they usually went to stay with my father when their boarding schools closed.

Mama, I'm going to spend some time talking about my father now. Even as an adult, I am still quite emotionally removed and uncertain when it comes to talking about my relationship with my father. He was kind to me, maybe even loving, but I was never able to form the same kind of attachment with him as I did with you. He probably damaged me more than you did, but my heart does not cling to him. I do not fight to disentangle myself from him, because I forgave and let him go a long time ago. I do not feel his life and death in my bones as I do yours.

Not to say that I did not love my father. I had a lot of admiration for him. He was highly successful as a businessman, had a lot of friends, and a lot of confidence. He provided a lifestyle that was enviable, and was more generous with his kindness and affection.

Mama, my father was the epitome of success in his home village. I was having a conversation with an older cousin recently, and he told me my father was the man that he wanted to be when he was a child. Living in the rural village in the 80s and early 90s, seeing a car was a rare thing. And so whenever my father came home with his car, it attracted villagers from all over. They showered him with praise and admiration, and he in turn made it rain cash, food, and drinks.

Being one of the older children in the family, and the only financially successful one at the time, he took it upon himself to pay for his siblings' schooling. He extended that generosity beyond his family to relatives and other people that came to beg for his help.

No doubt my father was a good man from the perspectives of many of the people he uplifted and supported.

My cousin told me that beyond being generous, my father was a hard worker, and he detested laziness in other people. Nothing annoyed him more than someone that was not willing to put in the work in order to be successful. My cousin said he admired this in my father as a child, and it inspired him to grow up to be the same. I listened to him and as much as I wanted to ask questions about how that was working out for him in his relationships, I chose to keep my comments to myself. He was right, my father was hardworking, very successful, but highly impatient and judgmental of people he perceived to be lazy. He was also generous to a fault, but his generosity was mostly felt outside of his immediate family.

I struggled to hear the praises that my cousin was heaping on my father. It was especially hard because it came at a time when I was feeling particularly upset about the effects of some of the choices he made, which continue to impact me today. Mama, as much as I say that I have forgiven my father and let him go, I still have moments of resentment and wishing he had made different choices.

My father was a violent man. Not to me. He never raised a violent hand on me as far as I can remember. But I saw him beat you almost to death, and he did the same to some of my siblings. I never felt that I could trust him not to seriously hurt or kill me if I ever made him angry enough. To me, he was a beloved but deeply feared father.

Lucky for me, I was a "good child", and I never did anything bad enough to awaken his wrath. Mama, my father was harder to upset than you were. Maybe because he was not around much and didn't get to see the smaller day to day mistakes that we made. Only the bigger things were visible to him, and given my introverted and secretly fearful nature, I did not tend to get involved in any kind of trouble that was big enough to get his attention.

The Beginning of a New Life

Moving to Kisumu marked the beginning of a new life for me. The silence was broken. The house was large, and bright, and seemed to have a life of its own. The first day or two of being there, I got lost trying to find my way around. I would forget which way I went to get to the upstairs balcony, or which bathroom I'd been to that had the fresh smelling air freshener. There was no yelling, no unexpected angry outbursts, no illness, no foul-mouthed neighbors.

My father bought us new clothes, and anything else that we needed. We had two houseboys who kept the house clean, cooked our food, reminded us to shower, and played with us. It was a different life than what we were used to.

I was deeply aware though that you were still sick at the hospital. My father hardly ever talked about you. My sister, Lena, was with you at the hospital, and my father visited once in a while. I asked him once if we could come and visit you. He said no. I never asked again, not because I didn't want to, but because you had raised me to accept the feedback I was given by an adult without ever daring to question it.

I heard him say once that your brother was trying to push him to move you to a hospital in Nairobi, where you would receive better medical care. But he thought it was a bad idea, because you would probably not survive the journey.

I don't remember my sister, Lena, ever coming home during the time you were at the hospital. She stayed with you throughout your time there, everyday by your side. Mama, I will tell you more later about my relationship with Lena now. But I think a lot about the months that she spent with you at the hospital, how totally devastating that must have been for her. She has never talked to me directly about that. But your sister, Robina, told me about your last days. She was not there with you, but Lena was more likely to talk to her about you than she was to talk to me.

My father hardly ever came to visit you. And when he did, there was very little warmth, or concern. That hurt you. You felt that other people, who were further removed from you, and from us as a family, showed you more care than he did. One of my father's younger brothers, for example, went out of his way to show concern during your illness. His wife was a former student of yours, and you actually introduced them to each other. This uncle traveled all the way from Nairobi to come visit you at the hospital, in that small town of Bungoma, for no reason at all, other than to see how you were doing. It must have been a deeply painful time in your life, Mama. I imagine you must have felt lonely, and hurt by my father's behavior. Not to mention that your children were not allowed to come and see you.

You might be pleased to learn, Mama, that this particular uncle actually named his daughter, who was born about a year after your passing, after you. He gave her both of your names.

You cried a lot in your last days. Your heart broke for your children. One time, you had a dream that you died, and when you got to the next world, you saw your mother.

Your mother died a few years before I was born. I didn't know a lot about her, but from what I've gathered over the years, she had you and a few of your siblings with a man she met after separating from her first husband. She later returned to her first husband's home, where your brothers later settled. I have never seen any pictures of your father, Mama, and I know close to nothing about him. It is suspected though that that is where you got your light skin complexion, which you passed on to me. I've heard speculation that he might have been a man from a different community. I'm mildly curious about that sometimes, although having that information would probably not make any difference to me anyway.

Aunt Robina told me the story of your mother's passing. It was two or three years before I was born. Your family seemed to attract envy from the neighbors because you and your siblings were doing things to make your mother's life easier. On the day she died, your mother woke up healthy, with no indication at all that anything was wrong. She went about her day as usual, taking care of the home. You had come to visit, and the rest of your siblings were there too. For some reason, some sodas were bought, and you had a little family time with your mother and your siblings.

Robina said the presence of sodas at your family table was a cause for envy and bitterness amongst some neighbors. It was a general feeling of "how dare you drink sodas when the rest of us are drinking porridge?" Petty as it may sound, it was a real issue for some people, at least according to Aunt Robina.

That evening, your mother suddenly fell seriously ill. She lay in bed shivering, and could not speak at all. It was strange and unexplainable. That night, when she got up to go relieve herself outside, she collapsed and died on the spot.

Your family was devastated by the loss of your mother. Aunt Robina still believes it was witchcraft. She recounted this story to me again recently, and I wanted to reach out and hug her. Mama, your sister is probably the closest I can ever come to having even the slightest bit of you back in my life again. She has a lot of stories to share about you. She loves you deeply. Sometimes I am too afraid to ask her about you. Hearing her talk about you fills me up with joy and longing, which is usually followed by a consuming sense of emptiness.

In your own deathbed, you saw your mother. She was not happy to see you there, in the afterlife, at all because it meant that your children were orphaned. She spoke sternly and asked you whom you had left your children to.

That dream gave you a lot of distress. There seemed to be a belief that if you were nearing death, and you had a dream like that where your dead loved one spoke to you, it meant you were actually going to die. You cried for us, Mama, and begged my sister to take care of your children when you were gone. She was maybe seventeen or eighteen years old at the time.

Mama, I have spent a lot of time in the years since your passing thinking about your last days; how painful and scary they must have been. I both envy and feel sorry for my sister that she walked that journey with you. Envy because the experience must have brought you two so much closer to each other, and sorry because I cannot imagine how difficult it must have been to watch you fade away, knowing that there was nothing she could do to save you.

I was never allowed to visit you again after that final time during our move to Kisumu. I regret that you had to endure the last few months of your life without seeing your children. I regret that I did not say anything the last time that I saw you. I could have touched you, hugged you, even if you could not hug me back. I could have said goodbye, and I didn't.

I am ashamed that I did not spend a lot of time thinking about you when you were in hospital. I was soaking in my new environment. I was making a lot of new friends at home and at my new school. I was starting to peek out of my shell of silence. I was nine years old, and I felt more aware of myself than I had ever felt before. I felt like a person, like I could do things, go places, and have friends. I could spend the night at a neighbour friend's house and nobody would even ask me about it. My father came home late most nights, and he wouldn't know whether or not I spent the night at home anyway. None of us reported things to him the way we used to report to you. Maybe it was fear, or maybe it was simply the fact that he was almost never home.

My life was changing, and while I was very aware that you were seriously ill, I was not overly concerned about it. In my logical mind, I knew there was the possibility that you could die, because I had heard that word mentioned in conversation about you a few times before, but somehow, I did not really see death as something that could actually happen to our family. You had vomited a bucket full of blood before and survived. You had been sick for a long time, and I hadn't seen you die yet. Deep down I knew it was coming, but at the same time, I did not believe it was actually possible for my mother to die.

Something is not Right

Mama, do you believe in intuition? I came home for lunch one day, and my heart was uneasy. My school was relatively far from our house, but we always came home for lunch, mostly because that is what the majority of other students at school did. A few people brought packed lunch, but there was nowhere to warm it, and cold food was not something I was particularly interested in. Other children bought food at roadside kiosks. I liked that option, and I did that once in a while, but our houseboy did not like the idea of making lunch only for us to fail to show up to eat it. He was always threatening to tell my father if we failed to come home for lunch. We had no choice but to come home, because if he did indeed tell my father we didn't come home for lunch, we would have the difficult task of explaining what we ate and where we got the money to buy that food. My father was not very careful with his money. Sometimes we did take coins that he left lying around in his room.

That afternoon, my heart kept fluttering in my chest. I got sudden feelings of panic, like something bad was about to happen. It was a bit of a familiar feeling though that I experienced whenever my father raised his voice, or whenever I sensed his anger. When my father was home, if I heard as much as the slamming of a door, I panicked, and this often left a kind of physical pain in my chest.

But my father was not home. And I was getting that feeling of panic. I had a dull pain in my chest that would not go away.

The phone rang. Our houseboy ignored it. He was setting the table for lunch and hustling us to come eat quickly so we would not be late going back to school. He was a small bodied young man with a face that looked like it had been carefully chiseled to achieve perfect angles at every corner. He did smile once in a while, but his default face was a serious and stern one. We did not fear him though. He was a nice young man that was full of threats that he never followed through with.

The phone rang again. It was one of those old landline phones that made a loud shrill sound that was somewhat hard on the ears. We were quite proud of it though. Prior to moving to Kisumu, I had never seen a telephone and did not know any family that owned one.

The phone kept ringing until the houseboy got annoyed and picked it up. There was irritation in his voice when he answered.

"Hello?" He frowned.
The person on the other side spoke for what seemed like an extended period of time. The houseboy periodically said a muffled yes, but was otherwise quiet. The dull pain in my chest came alive and a gush of blood seemed to suddenly rush to the area. My heart was pounding, frantically trying to make sense of what was happening.

I tried to read the houseboy's face. I could see that something was wrong.

"When?" He asked.

He listened quietly again for what seemed like a long time. I could not hear anything of what the caller was saying. Finally, he thanked the caller and hung up the phone.

"Who was that?" I asked.

"Nobody," he said and walked out of the room.

My brothers seemed oblivious to whatever was going on. I was sure that something was wrong, and deep down I knew exactly what it was. But I dared not say anything.

"Eat your food and go to school," the houseboy yelled from the kitchen. "I don't want you to be late going back to school."

I wanted to ask him again who had called, but I could not. I was not the kind of child that pushed adults after I had already been given an answer. In truth, I was not even sure I wanted to hear what the young man had been told on the phone at that moment. My heart was not ready. So I ate what I could get down from what was on my plate, and went back to school.

The feeling of panic persisted. I could not concentrate in class. After the first afternoon lesson, I could not take it any longer. I took my bag, sneaked out of class and hid in the pit latrines at the edge of the field. I was not the kind of student that skipped class, let alone run away from school. But the pain in my chest was not letting up, and I felt that I had to go home. I could definitely not make it to the end of the school day. Everything in me was pushing me towards home.

From the pit latrine, I watched the gate, looking for an opportunity to escape. There was no way I was going to go through that gate unnoticed. So I opted for the fence. A gap in the barbed wire fence behind the storeroom seemed like a safer bet. Some students used it to escape and go home early after classes so they wouldn't have to stay for co-curricular activities. I had never done it before myself, but I knew exactly where and how to do it.

I got out of school unnoticed. I could not use the normal path home, because I was afraid I would meet someone that would then report me to the school or to my father. So I took a different route home.

The path was confusing, and muddy. I was not very familiar with it despite having used it a few times with some friends. I thought it would be easy to find my way home, but I ended up lost. I kept walking back and forth, making my way forward, realizing I was not on the right path, making my way back, and trying to figure out the way again. In my confusion, I stepped into a pool of mud and lost one of my shoes. I tried to dip my hand into the mud to find it, but realized I was only making a bad situation worse by making myself all muddy. So I left my lost shoe behind and continued walking with one shoe.

I felt tears burn in my eyes. I did not cry easily, except when

I was beaten. I understood physical pain, and I reacted to it appropriately. But crying because I was lost and my shoe was stuck in the mud, that was out of my range of normal.

I might as well have stayed in school. Other children coming from school found me wandering around trying to find my way to the main road. I did not ask them for directions, but I followed them, knowing that they had to be going in the general direction that I needed to go. When my father first enrolled us in that school, he dropped us off on the first day and never set foot in the school again. It was assumed we would find our own way home and would be able to make our way there every morning henceforth. I had never up until that point fully understood the paths. Every morning, and every evening, I relied on secretly following other children in school uniform to ensure that I did not get lost.

Walking in the general direction that other children were walking got me to the main road, and from there, I found my way home easily.

As soon as I got to the gate, my younger brother came out running. He was in lower primary and did not have classes in the afternoons. He only attended school until lunch time.

"Mami!" He yelled, "Do you know that Mama is dead?"

I walked past him without acknowledging him at all.

In my heart, I already knew that you were dead. Hearing my brother say it gave me a bit of a jolt. But I did not react. I barely looked at him.

There was a small crowd of people in our house, none of whom I knew. When I walked in, they all turned to look at me. I froze for a second, staring back at them and not knowing what to do with myself. Recovering quickly, I politely half waved at them and ran up the stairs.

The room that I shared with my sisters was also full of women. I dropped my bag at the door and walked in. My sister Lena was on the bed, propped in the arms of a woman that I knew to be the wife of my father's best friend. Her name was Mrs. Maina. She was a nurse and was probably one of the most confident mothers I knew. She was solid, held her space with no apologies, and always seemed to know what to do in whatever situation. When she visited our house, she did not sit down timidly like most visitors did. She was right at home every time, and she took herself to any space in the house as though she actually lived there. Her children were equally confident. They seemed to feel more at home in our home than even we did.

"Come here," Mrs. Maina said, reaching out to me with one arm. I walked over and she pulled me in for a hug.

I let her hug me, but awkwardly and stiffly stood there, not sure whether it would be appropriate to return the hug. Any show of affection felt unnatural to me. She let me go and went back to comforting my sister. Lena had clearly been crying for a while and was exhausted from it.

I walked out of the room and into my father's bedroom. My father was sitting on his bed, head resting in the palm of his right hand. He reached out with his arm and I walked over to him. He seemed exhausted too. I sat next to him on the bed, mud and all.
"Mami," he said, pulling me in and holding me close to him.

He was quiet for a while. I had never seen my father like that before. He looked beaten, confused, and was nowhere near the self-assured, always in control father that I knew.

"Mami," he said again, and turned to look me in the eyes, "your mother has gone to be with the Lord."

I said nothing. No kind of reaction was forthcoming. I did not know what to do with myself other than sit there quietly and awkwardly.

I sat with my father for a while. My younger brother came to join us. I could hear Lena crying on and off in the next room, and women begging her to hush. Lena's sobs were the only indications that something was wrong. My mind was empty, my chest pains were gone, everything was just there, meaningless. It felt like being a piece of furniture in the room, just existing and feeling nothing. My father said some things to us, none of which I remember. I sat quietly on his bed and listened to the sound of my sister's crying without thinking anything of it.

One Last Time

The next few days were a blur. I retreated into myself. I could not stand the amount of wailing and activity that was happening around me. Your sisters irritated me. The day they arrived at our house, they started wailing before they even got to the gate. I could not understand why they needed to do that. They were calling attention to our family, which is something I would have wanted to avoid.

I hated that they had to hug me and cry in my ear, and that they spent the nights crying and lamenting. It felt like they never slept. They were constantly either crying or telling stories about you, which would lead to even more crying.

I was highly irritable. I did not react to the many annoyances around me, but in my heart I hated just about everybody that came to our house. Any crying especially, greatly upset me. I spent most of the days hiding in my father's bedroom. Our own room was always swarming with female relatives.

Much as I tried, I could not bring myself to cry. I wanted silence. The noise and activity around me was overwhelming.

Mrs. Maina and my father's office secretary took us shopping for funeral clothes. We ended up with some red clothes for the girls, complete with matching hats, and suit pants, shirts, and bowties for the boys. My dress was red, but different from my sisters' outfits. It was a little bit exciting to have new clothes, but the excitement was diluted by everything else that was happening at home.

The journey to our rural home in Kisii was exhausting. A whole caravan of cars, most belonging to my father's friends, accompanied us. He seemed to have a lot of rich friends. My father traveled in the hearse, with the casket containing my mother's body. The hearse arrived from Bungoma and the caravan immediately started moving. There was no time to even notice what was going on. My siblings and I all got separated into separate cars. It was believed that it is bad luck for entire families to travel in one vehicle when going to a funeral.

Your sisters did their usual thing as we were getting settled into the cars. I wanted to scream at them to stop. Their wailing was irritating and distressing for me. But who was I to speak? I endured it and prayed it would be over soon.

Once we got to the shopping center near our rural home, we were greeted by a massive crowd of mourners who surrounded the cars and started wailing through the windows. It was like a scene from an apocalyptic nightmare. People were staring at me, talking to me in Kisii, and telling me things I could barely understand. I stared back at them and said nothing. I just wanted the whole thing to be over.

As soon as we got out of the vehicles, I went to find my siblings. My brothers and I were ushered to a bench under a tree as the mourners followed the casket to the front of our rural house. It was an old mud house with an iron sheet roof that still seemed to be in pretty good shape. My family had lived there when I was born, and only moved to Busia when I was around two years old.

The whole homestead was a beehive of activity for hours. It sounded like a storm, with low moans, high pitched screams, and everything in between. Your oldest brother was walking around the compound sobbing and shouting, repeating over and over that they had brought him someone else's body, that the body in that casket was not his sister.
I had never met your oldest brother before. But I had heard a lot of stories about him. Rumor had it that he was completely normal until his wife gave him a love potion called *kababa*, which is supposed to make a man settle down at home and stop roaming around and causing trouble for his wife. However, it was also known to make some men docile to the point of becoming imbeciles. Word around was that this uncle had been unlucky enough to be negatively impacted by the *kababa* his wife fed him. He was now highly docile, and slightly out of his mind. Everything I had heard about him suggested that he was incapable of having a normal relationship with people, and so I was not surprised that I had never met him before, and that even

at the funeral, he never came over to say a single word to us. He mourned you nice and proper, openly and without any shame, but he did not seem aware that you had children, and did not in any way acknowledge our presence.

Your sisters-in-law, the wives of my father's brothers, were running up and down trying to get things done. They had cooked a lot of food and were busy making sure the visitors from out of town were fed and had a place to sit. My sisters disappeared into one of the houses. They were more familiar with the home, and with the relatives, and so it was easy for them to blend right in. My brothers and I on the other hand were confused and overwhelmed. We sat under the tree for what seemed like hours. Somehow, everyone seemed to have forgotten about us, except for the local mourners that kept coming over to stare at us and converse in Kisii about how young the children you had left behind were.

I heard your name a lot that day. It was ringing in the air. Everywhere I turned someone was screaming your name. Mama, you were loved, deeply, by so many people. It was good for me to see that, to be reminded that you had such a rich life, and such deep relationships, before the sadness and depression took you over.

Later in the evening, when the activity had begun to die down and the mourners were leaving the compound, I went to find my father. He was sitting next to the casket. His eyes were bloodshot and slightly swollen. I could not imagine my father crying, but

he looked like he had been crying. He asked if I wanted to see your body. I nodded my head, yes.
You looked nothing like yourself. Your face was shrunken, wrinkled, and dry. It looked like the last drop of moisture had been sucked out of your body. I could see why your brother would be convinced it was not you in that casket. Maybe he was not that insane after all, because the woman in that casket was a far cry from the mother that I knew. I didn't doubt it was you, even though the body looked like that of a person that had been dead a long time. Your once light caramel skin had turned into a dark mass of dry, crumbled flesh. The dryness and wrinkles on your face were so extreme it was as though your body had been left out in the sun to dry to a crisp.

You were dressed like a bride; a white gown, with a beautiful veil on your head. At least someone had tried to make you look good. I stared at your gown. I wanted to touch it, but there was a glass partition that prevented that possibility. It was the first time I was seeing a dead body, but I was not afraid.

It was only my father and I in the room, and so I was able to take a fairly good look before stepping away from the casket. I wish I had looked longer, taken in more of you before you were permanently lowered into the ground. I guess I imagined that there would be other opportunities to see you again before that happened. And so I stepped away, pulled a stool, and sat next to my father until someone came to get me so I could eat something.

My siblings, a few cousins, and I all slept in a house belonging to one of my uncles. He was a delightful man with a big personality, but he had a reputation for being short tempered. He'd brought home a record number of wives (more than ten, from what I heard), and none of them lasted long enough for any of us to meet her twice. He beat each of them almost to death and replaced them soon after. One of them discovered that he had another wife after he had already brought her home, and when she inquired about it, she got the beating of her life, and was left with blood oozing out of her ears. Another one had just returned home after giving birth at the hospital, and even before she had time to catch her breath, she got a ruthless beating for one reason or the other.

These were all well known stories about my uncle, but looking at him, and hearing him talk, one could not imagine him hurting a fly. I was quite fond of him because of his humor. He was a smooth talker, and his personality was a magnet. Everyone that did not know him well thought he was the most charming person in the world. His presence lit up the room, and one couldn't help but want to be around him to hear his marvelous stories. On the surface, the stories we heard about him did not seem to align with the man that we found so entertaining and loveable.

The next morning was the day of your burial. I woke up early and went to our house to check on my father. He was sitting outside as one of his younger brothers, the one that had traveled from Nairobi to see you at the hospital, dug a hole in front of our house. I learned that the hole he was digging was actually your grave. It was right at the doorstep of the house. The casket was inside. My father had slept alone in our house with the casket. He looked sad, and exhausted. I sat with him, watching my uncle dig your grave. The story was that this uncle had failed to show up to a few funerals that he was supposed to have attended, and as punishment, he was given the choice to either get flogged by his relatives, or dig your grave by himself. He chose to dig the grave.

It did not occur to me to view your body one last time. I thought the day was still young, and that you would be around for a while longer. But everything happened in one quick flash. I have no recollection of anything that was said at your burial ceremony. I wore my oversized red dress with the matching hat and sat quietly at the front row, together with my siblings. Your casket was on a table under a small makeshift structure that was made out of tree logs and bamboo mats.

Before I even realized what was happening, the ceremony was over. My brothers were ushered away quickly, and while I didn't think much of it at that moment, I later came to find out that they had been taken to the graveside to throw some earth into your grave. My sisters and I were never given that opportunity. I did not even get to see your casket lowered to the ground. One moment we were all sitting down listening to speeches, and the next thing I knew, your grave was already filled with earth and a wooden cross was sticking awkwardly on top of it.

Tiny Waterfalls

The days after your funeral were quiet. Your sisters came to visit everyday. They brought food, helped clean the compound, and spent time with us. They were very present, and they were not wailing anymore. The quiet was a welcome change from the chaos of the weeks before. Nobody was talking about you. When your sisters came over, they were happier, and more interested in gossiping about my father's family than talking about your lives together. I found this to be a relief, and I liked them better that way.

There was speculation about whether or not my father would remarry. My sister Lena said that she hoped he wouldn't. Aunt Robina got quite defensive and went on a bit of a rant about why marrying another woman is not the worst thing that could happen. She was a second wife herself, and was therefore sensitive to the topic of that discussion.

I wondered what I felt about my father possibly getting remarried. The evil stepmother was a common theme in many of the children's stories I heard and read when I was in lower primary. I could not imagine a stepmother being anything but wicked and conniving. But I did not have the space in my mind to worry about my father's next steps in the marriage department. I was too busy filling my mind with juicy gossip about relatives

I barely even knew.

I was meeting most of my extended family for the first time. Mama, your family was more sober and had fewer insane characters. Save for your oldest brother, whose wife had allegedly destroyed his mind with *kababa*, the rest of your siblings were fairly level-headed. Aunt Rebecca was mostly introverted, but she had a beautiful smile, a gentle stare, and could be a springfield of affection sometimes. The brother that was your immediate follower in birth order was good friends with my father. I wondered how he felt about how my father treated you. If he had any opinions about it, he never made them known to us. He was soft spoken, and fairly present in our lives. Your youngest brother was one we feared. He lived with us in Busia for an extended period of time at some point and was never shy about using the stick on our behinds and tiny legs whenever we did anything wrong. He was even more enthusiastic about beating us than you were. Aunt Robina was the youngest in your family, and the most loving. To date, she still adores you and speaks about you as though you were an angel in human flesh.

My father's family on the other hand had all kinds of crazy characters. They were big personalities, and they fought at the slightest provocation, with each other, with their wives, and with just about anybody they could find a reason to fight with. The family was divided into various camps, with some people getting along fine, and others being enemies. It was said that the parents also had favorites, and this contributed to the family divide. My father was a favorite of his mother. He looked very much like her, and I guess it helped that he had money.

My grandfather was a little bit more removed from the family drama, but there was the story about the curse he placed on my father. Some years before, when our family still lived in Kisii, my grandfather got upset with my father for some reason, and the two had an argument. I never understood what the argument was about, but it ended in a curse. My grandfather said my father's children would grow to be crooks. The Kisii word that he used could mean anything from simply hard-headed to toughened crooks. Mama, I don't know what kind of father curses his own children, but this man cursed not one, not two, but almost all of his children. What I came to learn about him is that his mother died giving birth to him, and that he had quite a traumatic childhood. I don't know how true that story is, but it gave me a better understanding of his emotional distance from his own family.

My father moved our family away after falling out with his father. Over the years after that, their relationship was cold but cordial. My grandfather came to visit once in a long while, but he hardly seemed interested in us or our lives. He could never remember my name. At best, he would be able to guess correctly that I was my father's daughter. But he did not know my name and he was not keen to find out anything about me.

Some members of the community were also said to practice

witchcraft. My own father believed in witchcraft, and although he didn't practice it himself, as far as I knew, he was known to consult witchdoctors when things went wrong in his life. I saw him bring a witchdoctor home when you were unwell, and a few times after your death as well. Night running was another trait that was associated with a few women in the immediate community, but no one dared talk about it too loudly. It was a secret, but a very well known one.

My sisters told us stories about when our family still lived in Kisii. The night runners would entertain themselves by terrorizing families at night. They threw stones on the roofs, knocked on doors and windows, made weird noises, and generally made it impossible for their victims to sleep in peace.

Night runners were believed to be harmless for the most part. They only became dangerous when one tried to catch them or interfere with their nocturnal activities. If one accidentally or intentionally ran into a night runner when they were in their night running persona, the person risked getting their memory wiped or losing their ability to speak forever. It was therefore advisable to stay out of their way and never try to catch one.

Some night runners were said to have the ability to summon people from their sleep and make them join their activities. The summoned person would be made to carry the night runner on their backs and run with them from home to home as they went about their usual work. And in the early dawn, when it was time to go back home, the summoned person would find their way home, get back in their beds, and have no memory whatsoever of what happened during the night. Their bodies would be tired and sore from all the running, but they would not remember leaving their house at all.

These stories were fascinating to me. They gave color to my sense of self, even though I had little connection to either side of my extended family, and had zero desire to be associated with the darkness some of them represented. Somehow though, the craziness made me feel like I had some depth, and some richness to my history.

My cousins and I spent the days exploring the countryside. We went to the farms, ate sugarcane, and plucked tea leaves. We also discovered the river where some people went to bathe in the outdoors, while others went to wash clothes, or simply fetch water to take home. The water was clean and fresh, and it ran against rocks that were stunningly beautiful. You could see the river for a long stretch as it came down the slope. Some parts of it looked like tiny waterfalls. I had never seen anything like it in my life.

Sometimes I went down to the river by myself, sat there for hours just watching those tiny waterfalls. They were beautiful, and peaceful. I would take off my shoes, stand on the rocks and let the water roll through my feet.

Village life was magical. At night we sat around the fire, roasting maize, and listened to my uncles' stories. They were hilarious. Most of my father's brothers were younger than him, and nothing like him. My father was serious and more grown up in the way he presented himself, while most of his brothers were playful, funny, and more carefree. I have no idea what my father did with his time while we were at the village. He never joined us for meals, or for the evening stories by the fireside. Every time I looked for him, I found him sitting alone inside or outside our old mud house. He seemed genuinely broken by your death.

What it's Like to Have a Best Friend

We went back to school. That was the hardest part about life after your funeral. My classmates looked at me funny, they didn't know how to behave around me or what to say. I also did not know what to say to them. I simply went back to class and shut everyone out. Some girls tried to talk to me, but it always came across as pity, and I did not need that at all. Some asked me questions about you. I completely refused to talk about you. Instead I smiled at people when I couldn't talk to them, or otherwise kept to myself.

There was one girl in my class that was the exception to my keeping to myself tendencies. I walked home with her every day. She was a tiny girl with big, beautiful eyes and skin as dark as night. I had no idea where she lived, or why she liked me, but she waited for me every day and walked with me all the way home before proceeding to her own house. We played games on the way, picked wildflowers, talked about our teachers, and the other girls in our class. She never once asked me about you, or told me sorry for losing you. For that reason alone, she was the only person I opened myself up to in my class. She was the only one that got anything more than a cold smile and a cold shoulder from me at school.

It was at home though that I found my first real friend, Peace. She went to the same school I did. But she was about two years younger, and therefore two grades behind me. That meant that I almost never saw her at school. She was in lower primary, and as such did not have classes in the afternoons.

Although she was only seven years old, and I was nine, Peace and I understood each other very well. Her house was identical to ours and stood right in the next compound. I believe both were rented from the same owner. Her mother was a nice, quiet woman, and she had no problem with me spending large amounts of time at their place. I spent the night with them sometimes, and Peace spent the night at our house too every now and then. We were like sisters, although she was nothing like my sisters. My sisters were much older than I was, and I had very little in common with them. Lena was in college, and Bonareri was in a boarding high school.

I was very lonely. My brothers and I did not grow up playing together. There was an unspoken gender divide, and we fought more than we were nice to each other. I felt very much alone in the world.

A young man in our house, whose name I cannot bring myself to mention (even though it's been decades) sexually abused me on occasion. He never penetrated me, but he would sneak into my room and rub himself on me when he thought I was asleep. I endured it, pretending to be asleep, and never gave any indication that I knew what he was doing to me. He had done the same thing to me numerous times before, including when you were still alive.

Mama, this was the third scene that my mind took me to during my hypnosis session. I saw myself on the bed, my eyes wide open, and my body stiff. I felt this man behind me, fumbling in the sheets to pull my dress up and my underwear down. I described this to the therapist, and even in that hypnotic state, I felt her jolt. Maybe the scene touched a raw nerve for her, but I felt that she was taking this scene more personally than the previous ones. She got protective and angry at what was happening to me.

The memory was not painful for me to describe. In fact, none of the scenes I described in my hypnosis were painful. I realized that I had reached a point in my healing when telling my story was no longer something that triggered pain, or anger. I felt somewhat removed from the experience, as though it had happened in another life.

I was tempted to tell Peace about the abuse. Though younger in age, Peace knew more about most things than I did. She was very confident and outspoken. She had conversations with adults as though she was one of them. I was painfully shy. I wanted to tell her so that she could tell me it was normal, that I didn't have to worry about it. But I already knew it was not normal, and it was not the kind of thing you just told someone. And so I kept it to myself until it finally stopped when our houseboy got promoted to office assistant at my father's office, and we got a housegirl. The young man's attention shifted from me to the housegirl.

Mama, it's been decades since this happened, but until recently I had only ever been able to tell my husband and one friend about it. This year, my sister Lena and I had a slight breakthrough in our difficult relationship, and I ended up telling her about the abuse. We were speaking on the phone. When the words came out of my mouth, I instantly felt relief, because finally someone that knew this person knew about what happened to me all those years ago.

There was a brief moment of silence, and then Lena opened up and told me even more about my own abuse than I had previously known. She told me that when I was a baby, you caught this same person touching me inappropriately and trying to do things to me. The person was a child too at the time, but he was old enough to know what he was doing. You were horrified, of course, and you told my father about it. The person was given some kind of punishment, and that was the end of that. Nobody ever talked about it again.

I assume that this person continued to abuse me as a baby, because he did it throughout whatever I can remember of my childhood. He would touch me and rub himself on me at night, and then in the morning, he would act like nothing had happened.

None of my siblings knew about it, and even now, as I gather the courage to put it on here, I do not know that I can sit down with them to talk about this. I talked to Lena about it on the phone, and it was like unloading a burden I had carried for many years, but even with her, I discussed it casually and dismissed it as nothing.

I think about this young man (not young at all anymore) and I wonder why he did what he did to me. Does he know that I remember? Does he wonder if I have told anyone about it? We still talk to each other once in a while, but our relationship is obviously strained and distant. I have thought about putting him on blast for what he did to me, but I cannot do that because he has children, and his children do not deserve to live with the sins of their father. Publicly calling him out on it would also certainly not change anything for me. The only thing that would do is to disrupt his life, and cause unrest in my extended family. None of that will change any of what happened to me.

Mama, after my conversation with Lena, I tried to figure out how I felt about the fact that you knew what this person was capable of. You found him abusing me as a baby, and he continued to abuse me right under your nose. I could not say anything to you about it because you were always angry, and I definitely could not say anything to my father because he was barely ever at home. And even if he were more present, how would I even say something like that to my father? Where would I start? I was too ashamed to admit to myself that it was happening, let alone tell anyone.

Mama, I have no answer to the question of how I feel now about what Lena told me. I have no blame left to dish out. The only thing left to seek is peace and healing.

There was some comfort that came with having a friend. My inner world was tumultuous and messy, but on the outside I maintained a protective silence. Peace would speak on both of our behalfs when we were with other people. She was very protective and told people off when they asked me questions I did not want to answer. The most common question I got from other girls our age was about my mother. I never asked Peace to protect me from that, but somehow she understood my discomfort around the topic and would quickly jump in to dismiss the question so I wouldn't have to answer it.

Peace witnessed a lot of happenings in our house. She was like part of the family. She saw and heard things, but she didn't dwell on any of it or ask for explanations. She didn't pity us, or judge us. She never even told me sorry when I lost you. She was just present, and that was all I needed from her.

One night, she was sleeping over at our house. As was usually the case with him, my father came in the dead of night and honked his car horn several times at the gate. Our houseboy was not around that day. My oldest brother, Paul, and my cousin (the son of Mr. Maina, my father's best friend) were sleeping in the guest room downstairs. I heard the honking but didn't get up because it was never my responsibility to open the gate when my father came home. My father honked and honked, each honk angrier than the last. I wanted to go down the stairs and wake my brothers up, but I was paralyzed with fear because of the impatience and growing anger I could sense in my father. Eventually my father got out of his car and started banging on the gate.

Peace and I both sat up on the bed. My heart was racing. The banging on the gate was so loud that it was impossible to imagine how my brother and cousin could not hear it. Peace and I looked at each other, and without speaking, we got out of bed, crept downstairs into the guest bedroom and woke my brother up.

Paul got up quickly, put on a shirt and went out to open the gate. Peace and I ran back upstairs and locked the bedroom door.

The moment the car was in the compound and the gate was closed, the slaps, kicks, and blows began. My father started beating my brother from outside the house. Paul ran into the house yelling. My father followed him into the guest bedroom without uttering a single word. That is how I knew things were serious. When my father got into his more serious episodes of rage, he hardly spoke, but the violence that came out of him was frightening.

We could hear things being thrown around, slaps, punches, screams. My cousin found himself thrown into the violence as well. We could hear both boys screaming in pain. My heart raced. My chest hurt. In my mind, I imagined that Paul was going to be dead soon. I was not sure my father was capable of stopping himself before causing serious damage.

In all honesty, the fear I felt listening to the beating my brother and cousin were receiving was more for myself than for them. For some reason, I had become a bit desensitized to my siblings, and most of what I felt was an instinct towards self preservation.

Peace and I sat quietly on my bed. Neither of us said a word.

The beatings went on for what seemed like a long time. When it was finally over, we heard my father coming up the stairs. I could feel my body shaking. He went into his room and closed the door. Peace and I both sighed with relief and lay back down on the bed.

I did not sleep that night. I wondered what was going through my father's mind. Was he drunk? Was he always going to be like that? Had we moved from my mother's momentarily painful physical abuse to my father's potentially deadly violence? Were we going to survive living with him?

Early the next morning, Peace woke up and went back to her house. We did not talk about what happened that night. She simply got up, asked if I would come to her house later, and left after I confirmed that I would try. I stayed in my room for as long as I could. When I got out and went downstairs, my father was sitting at the dining room table. I walked past him quietly, avoiding eye contact, trying to shrink myself as much as possible in the hopes that somehow he wouldn't see me.

"Mami," he called.
I froze.
"Come here."
I walked up to him. He lifted me onto his lap. I was around nine years old, tall and skinny, but could still fit nicely on his lap.
"How is school?" he asked.
"Fine." I said.
"Are you working hard?"
"Yes."
"Good," he said, "You are a good girl. Not like these other ones over here."

I sat quietly on his lap for a little while. When he finally put me down, I went into the kitchen to get myself some breakfast. My cousin had left to go back to his home first thing in the morning, and my brother did not come out of the guest room all day. I wondered what my cousin would say to his parents. Our fathers were best friends and were always together. If my father was drunk the night before, his father probably was too. They were inseparable, and from stories I heard, both had made a habit of engaging in behaviors that were difficult for their families.

That afternoon Peace and I were back to playing together. It was as though nothing had happened. For the first time in my life, I felt like someone truly understood me. We were very much in sync with each other. She understood my need to detach from the chaos around me and played along in my pretense that nothing was wrong. Or maybe she was too young to make sense of what she was seeing in my house. Either way, all that mattered to me was that she saw my family for the mess that it was and still wanted to be my friend.

Phobia

Mama, do you remember talking about our tribal community? I got a deep sense of pride about being Kisii from hearing you talk about it. I remember you telling my sisters they should never marry men from certain communities, and naming what sounded like disgusting stereotypes about those tribes. You made it sound like being a Kisii was the greatest blessing one could receive. And so I was very proud of myself. Mama, it is confusing to me too sometimes, but you both broke and built my self esteem. You made me feel like I had such a rich background, strong ancestry, and that because of that I was already somebody, while at the same time making me feel so small and insignificant.

I wanted to live up to the ancestry that I descended from. One of the biggest ways to prove that I was worthy of being a Kisii was through circumcision. When my two older brothers got circumcised, you were elated, and you sang their praises for being brave through the process of becoming men. They must have been around ten and twelve years old. They were taken to a hospital, and the report was that neither of them cried. They came home with *lessos* tied around their waist, and were quickly rushed to a vacant house at the far end of our row of houses. As a female, I was not allowed to see them until they healed.

Getting circumcised seemed like such an honor to me. Once the boys healed, their *lessos* were given to my two older sisters, and I was promised that when my younger brother got circumcised, I would get his *lesso*. In exchange, when my sisters and I got married in the future, the boys would receive the cows that our husbands brought as bride price. The trade was terribly unbalanced, but it made sense to me, and I looked forward to receiving my brother's *lesso* in exchange for my future husband's cows.

Mama, I knew that you were circumcised too, and so were my sisters. All of you claimed that you did not cry during the procedure. Unlike the boys, all of your circumcisions were done outside of a hospital, possibly by old village women that had never set foot in a classroom. But you were all very proud of your circumcision, and especially of the idea (I'm not sure anymore if it's a fact) that you were brave despite the pain.

I was quite disappointed when I did not get circumcised at the same time as my older brothers. I felt like I was ready, although in reality, I just really wanted to be considered a big girl, and to get your approval. I thought that as long as I went through it without crying, you would be proud of me. I wanted that desperately.

My time came after your death unfortunately. It was only about five months after we laid you to rest, and the idea came abruptly. My father sat me down one morning and told me that I was ready to become a big girl - a woman. He asked if I knew what that meant. I knew what that meant alright. You had prepared me well for it, and I knew that it was the only way I could ever be accepted as a woman, and potential wife, in the Kisii community.

I did not know much about marriage, but I knew that I did not want to miss out on the chance of getting a husband in future because of not getting circumcised. I also did not want to be called *egesagane*, a demeaning term used to refer to uncircumcised girls, any longer.

And so my father and I were very much on the same page about my readiness for this step. In my mind, every Kisii woman did it. And those women that did not were quite unlucky.

I was excited, and I couldn't stop bragging to my siblings that I was finally going to become a big girl. My sister Lena smiled quietly, like she often did, and told me not to do it. She did not say why, and I did not care. Wasn't she the same person that had for years bragged about her own circumcision? I was not about to start listening to new opinions now. She said I would regret it if I got circumcised, and left it at that. Of course I did not listen to her. I was sure she was either kidding, or trying to get me to do something that would make my father upset.

Lena was mostly quiet and distant. My relationship with my sisters was lukewarm at best. They were away in boarding schools or college most of my life. I did not really grow up with them being around much. As such, I was not close to them, and I did not see them as authority figures I needed to listen to, even though they were much older than I was.

My father woke us up in the middle of the night. I was disoriented, and not exactly sure what was happening. He said today was the day. My sister Bonareri and I hurriedly took a shower and got dressed.

I knew that I was supposed to get circumcised at some point, but now that the moment was here, I was nervous and panicky. My knees were weak. I was confused about why we had to go in the middle of the night. But I was also excited to prove that I was brave and to make my father proud.

There was a driver waiting outside. Bonareri was coming with me. I thought my father would come too, but he patted my back and told me I was going to be a big girl now, then retreated into

his bedroom.
We drove into the night.

I expected a hospital. True, my sisters were circumcised traditionally by village women, but that had happened years before, and since my brothers had gotten their cut in a hospital, I had assumed it would be the same for me. As we drove along, however, it became clear that we were not going to any hospital. We got off the main road and onto some narrow roads in a congested slum. There were rusted *mabati* houses everywhere. The streets were dark, and save for a homeless person here and there sleeping under a *kiosk*, there was not a soul in sight.

We pulled up in a dark alley. The driver got out, opened the car door for us, and led us to a row of *mabati* houses. We made two or three turns before getting to a worn out, rusty *mabati* structure at a corner. The driver knocked as quietly as he could. Without missing a beat, the door flew open in his face. It was as though the person on the other side had been waiting right at the door.

The driver talked to the woman briefly, and then walked away, leaving me and my sister confused, staring at an elderly woman with her full day clothes and head scarf on. She did not look like she had been sleeping.

"Come in," she said.
My sister and I started walking into the house but she indicated

for my sister to wait outside. She pulled me into the house. I was starting to feel uneasy about the way things were unfolding. The woman looked scary, and she was not particularly concerned with trying to calm my nerves.

"Do you have any underwear on?" she asked.
I nodded my head, yes. She told me to take it off and sit down.

There was a large piece of fabric on the floor. I sat down on it, my heart racing, my legs shaking.

Another elderly woman came from behind a curtain. She knelt down in front of me, pulled my dress up, and spread my legs. The first woman took a piece of cotton wool and wiped me. I shuddered and tensed up.

"I haven't even done anything yet," she laughed. "Sit still."

I saw her pick up a razor blade. My heart was pumping out of my chest. My entire body tensed up. The second woman went behind me, pinned my hands behind my back with her thighs and used her hands to spread out my legs.

"Now close your eyes," the first woman said.

I closed my eyes. I waited for something quick and painless to happen.

The woman pinched the tip of my clit. Before I could even wrap my mind around that, I felt a sharp pain that instantly hit every nerve in my entire body. The idea of being brave had no chance. It was worse than being stabbed in the throat. I felt pain on every inch of my existence, from the tip of my hair all the way to the edge of my longest toe nail. It was as though I had disappeared and my body was replaced by this excruciating, horrifying pain.

She took her time, slicing through my flesh, like a chef at a high end restaurant takes time to slice an expensive piece of steak that requires delicate precision. I screamed myself hoarse. I threw up in my mouth, swallowed my own vomit, and then screamed some more. The woman couldn't have been bothered. She carried right on while her colleague had me effortlessly pinned to the floor.

I fought with every inch of my being. But my effort was useless. My small frame stood no chance against the two women. I screamed until there was no more sound coming out of my mouth. It was like the dream where something dangerous is coming at you, and you feel like you are running, but you're actually not moving at all. Your body feels like it's fighting, but your arms and legs are not moving. I felt paralyzed.

When she was done, she put the piece of my flesh on a piece of tissue paper. She then took a large piece of cotton wool, shoved it in between my legs, and told me to stand up. I don't remember feeling pain at that point. I was just glad it was over. I pulled myself up, grabbed my underwear, and limped out behind her.

The driver appeared from around the corner just as we were coming out of the house. He did not look at me, or the elderly woman. I could tell that he understood what had just happened, and was too ashamed to acknowledge it, even through eye contact. He told my sister to follow him, and led us back to the car.

The elderly women did not say goodbye, or anything at all. They went back into the house and closed the door.

My sister started giggling when we got to the car. She said the whole town heard my screams, and that she couldn't believe how much I cried because of such a small thing. I told her to leave me alone. The driver pretended not to hear us. He kept his eyes on the road.

When we got home, it was still dark. My brothers were asleep, and my father was in his room. Lena opened the door for us and we made our way upstairs to our room. Traditionally, my father and brothers were not allowed to see me until after my wound healed.

Bonareri couldn't wait to share the whole story about how desperately I cried. She laughed and laughed, and made sure everyone heard about it. Lena took the kinder approach. She listened to the story but didn't laugh. I was probably too traumatized to do anything. I got into my bed and cried.

The cotton wool the woman put between my legs was soaked in blood. I tried to pull it off but part of it was stuck on my flesh. I thought for sure I was going to die. I cried so much I developed a fever and started trembling.

Lena was worried about me. She told my father I needed to go to the hospital, but when he responded with anger, asking her if she was the head of his family, my sister cowered and let the matter drop.

"I told you not to do it." She said as I lay trembling in my bed. Mama, I know that Lena was not my mother, and she was only about eighteen years old herself. But over the years I have asked myself what I would have done at that age if my father had tried to circumcise my little sister. If our roles were reversed, and knowing whatever Lena knew about the effects of what was happening, would I have been brave enough to stand up to my father? Would I have stayed home and let a stranger drive my little sister off to have her genitals mutilated?

I have also asked myself if it is fair for me to ask these questions. Regardless of what I would have done in her shoes, is it fair for me to judge the actions, or lack thereof, of an eighteen year old that was dealing with the trauma of losing her mother and living with a tyrannical step father?

Slowly but steadily, the wound started to heal. I stayed in my room, sleeping, crying, reliving the agony of what I'd experienced.

Then I convinced myself that it was okay. I was okay. I was finally a woman, and my father was going to be proud of me. That was all that mattered.

About a week after my circumcision, my sister Bonareri went out with my father to buy me new clothes. They brought me a purple skirt and a matching blouse, which I wore to come out of my room. It was the first time my father and brothers were seeing me in my new status as a 'woman'.

My father was beaming with pride. He held my shoulder and told me what a good job I did. At that moment, it all seemed like a bad dream that had finally come to an end. I was waking up to the love and approval of my father, and that seemed like the greatest reward anyone could give me.

I smiled sheepishly and let him lead me outside to the front yard of our compound. My sister brought a large cup of fermented milk, which my father proceeded to swoosh noisily in his mouth, before spraying the whole mouthful on my face. He recited some blessings in Kisii as he took another mouthful and repeated the process several times. I closed my eyes. It gave me joy to hear my father bless me in this 'after circumcision' tradition. I was proud of myself for making it through alive, and it almost didn't matter that I cried, that I was not as brave as I had imagined I would be.

In the weeks that followed, I became deeply aware that something had happened to my body that I could never undo.

My experiences of sudden panic intensified. I could not look at a knife, or any sharp object, without my skin crawling and my blood chilling. Even seeing a sharp object on TV triggered a panic reaction. This was not something that I could talk to anyone about. I was ashamed that I continued to be impacted so intensely by something that was supposed to be a good thing, a beautiful thing even. Rather than revel in my new found 'womanhood', I developed a phobia for sharp objects, which stayed with me long into my adulthood.

CHAPTER THREE

Dear Mama,

If there was one thing that my father did right, it was taking me to boarding school. It was hard, and painfully lonely, but it was what I needed in order to begin to grow into myself. I felt safe at school. I was not worried about what mood anyone would be in when they came home, and whether any given day was the day they were going to kill me. I could sit in my loneliness and be okay with it because I was not expecting anything bad to happen to me.

It was not hard for my father to sell the idea of boarding school to me. Not that my opinion counted for much, but when he mentioned it, I immediately jumped on the idea. My brothers were going to boarding school as well, so it did not make sense for me to be left behind. Living alone with my father was not an option. I wanted to experience life away from my family. In some ways, I felt trapped and caged in living at home. I felt unsafe, but without options.

I learned and grew a lot in boarding school. The journey was excruciatingly painful sometimes, but I truly believe boarding school saved my life.

The World Out Here

My father dropped me off at the school and left me in the care of my cousin, a form four (senior year) student at the high school. It was a girls only primary and secondary school. While the classroom sections of the two schools were separated, the dorms were in the same general area, and we shared a dining hall. I got to see my cousin several times throughout the day. She was pleasant, and nurturing, and so I went looking for her sometimes, even when I didn't really need anything.

I was assigned a school mother who was in grade eight, and I also had a school sister by virtue of sharing the same school mother. But since I had a cousin in the high school section, I did not rely much on the two.

Cousin Sheila was tall and curvy, slightly built, and was the kindest, most gentle grown person I had ever closely associated with. She was the daughter of Mr. Maina, my father's best friend. There was no blood relation between our two families, but Mr. Maina was the closest person to my father at the time, closer than his own family, and we naturally called his children our cousins. We did have some blood cousins scattered around the country, but I'd only ever met some of them at your funeral, and we did not have much of a relationship.

Sheila washed my clothes, made sure I ate at every meal, made sure I had everything I needed, and generally took care of me without expecting anything in return. There was really nothing I could do for her in return. I did not know how to do anything. I was not even good company. Every time I was with her, I was silent. I did what she asked me to do, handed her whatever she needed, but there was nothing I could talk to her about. I was like an empty shell, with gentle manners but no personality to speak of. I tended to shrink myself, afraid to take up space, almost apologetic for my own existence.

Some nights, she let me sleep with her in her dorm, sharing her bed. Most of those sleepovers were okay. I lay in her bed and listened to big girl talk as she chatted with the other high school girls. They did not mind having me around. One of her friends also had a cousin in the primary school, and the two of us became the adopted primary kids in that high school dorm. It felt good to spend time with the older girls. I admired their confidence and wanted to be just like them.

Once in a while, I accidentally wet Sheila's bed. I would wake up in the middle of the night, soaked in my own pee, and I would be greatly embarrassed because Sheila was soaked in my pee as well, and there was no way of hiding what I had done.

She was frustrated when that happened, but she never got overly upset with me, and never stopped inviting me over to sleep in her bed. She would just air the mattress out to dry, wash the bedsheets, and tell me to wake her up next time if I needed to go outside. There were no toilets in the dorms. One had to go outside and either walk about a couple of meters in pitch darkness to the toilets, or pee on the grass right outside the dorm. Both options were scary as hell, considering the many ghost stories I'd heard about the school, but wetting the bed was never intentional for me. I knew I could wake Sheila up if I needed to, and that would be so much easier for me than facing the embarrassment of peeing in my cousin's bed. But as much as I tried to avoid drinking water in the evenings, I still often woke up in a wet bed.

My school mother was also a kind older girl. She was in her final year of primary school, and I got the bunk bed directly above hers in the primary dorm. I spent some nights in my own bed, and quite a number of times, I peed in my mattress and some of it ended up on her bed since the mattress was so thin. She always responded kindly. She would help me take out my mattress so it could dry, and she taught me how to wash my bedsheets.

I had stopped wetting my bed at home, and so the recurrence of this in boarding school was quite distressing for me. At home, I would wet my bed maybe once in a long while, but at school it was as often as several times a week. One time, I wet myself in broad daylight, and right in front of all the girls in my class.

It was a weekend. Some girls were hanging out in the classrooms after lunch, having fun and telling stories. I was quite introverted, and while I enjoyed listening to other people's stories, I rarely had anything to contribute to the conversations. Soon I got tired and drowsy, so I lay down on the floor and fell asleep.

I slowly came awake to the sound of loud conversation. The girls were talking and laughing out loud as they exchanged stories and jokes. I was startled to realize that the floor around me was wet. No one seemed to be paying any attention to me, and so my first instinct was to sneak out of the classroom before anyone realized what had happened. But that was impossible. To get to the door, I would have to walk past the girls, and someone was bound to notice my soaked dress. Having ruled out the feasibility of that plan, I started to search my mind for an alternative explanation, something to convince myself and everyone else that I had in fact not wet myself in broad daylight. Maybe someone was playing a practical joke and had poured water on me as I slept?

I sat up with a bit of a scream, which drew everyone's attention. The girls asked what was wrong, and I said someone had poured water on me while I was sleeping. A number of girls walked over and surrounded me. One of them said she didn't think anyone poured water on me.

It was clear what had happened. My dress was wet, and the floor around me was wet. There were a good number of people in the room, and if someone had poured water on me, they would definitely have been seen.

I had never been more embarrassed in my life. My school sister, a small, talkative girl with a big personality, immediately jumped to my defense. She pointed out that she did believe someone poured water on me. She made a show of being upset and scolding the perpetrator, then pulled me up and walked me out of the classroom in dignity. At the dorm building, she got me some cold water in a basin, went with me to the bathrooms and stood there waiting as I took a bath. When I was done, she walked me back to the dorm, helped me find some clothes to change into, and protectively kept me by her side all day.

Everyone knew I had peed myself, but my school sister, tiny as she was, commanded respect among our peers. She made it clear, without having to actually say anything more, that no one was allowed to say a word about it. And so that was the end of that.

Mama, I was lucky to have people who liked me and looked out for me in that school. Maybe it's because I looked so fragile and quiet. My school sister was always trying to cheer me up. She was in my class, and although she did a lot of things for me that indicated her desire to be a good sister and friend, I remained aloof, mainly because I did not know how to deal with her bubbly personality. She would find me seated somewhere peacefully, then suddenly pull me up and start making me dance with her as she sang some song she liked about a woman called Rozy, which is also my English name. It was amusing, but also highly uncomfortable for me.

By the end of my second term in the school, the bedwetting had significantly reduced. I had settled in more, and I knew how to do some things for myself, like washing my own clothes. I understood the routines of the school and no longer needed as much of my cousin's help. I still spent a lot of time in her dorm, and slept over often, but I was also more independent now.

There was talk of ghosts lurking in the dark and waiting to grab a child at the slightest opportunity. The school, run mostly by Catholic nuns, was some decades old and was located in a rural village in Luo Nyanza. It was believed that whenever a priest or nun from the Parish died, they were buried at a cemetery nearby, and it was their ghosts that lurked in the dark shadows at night.

These stories terrified me. Sometimes when we were walking back to the dorms after night preps, the girls would suddenly take off running, screaming and claiming that someone had seen a ghost. I never saw one myself, but I would never be left behind when other people were running. I ran right along with everyone and often, when that happened, I would go straight to my cousin's dorm and sleep there.

In addition to the ghosts of the dead priests and nuns, we also had *nyawawa*, the evil spirits that traveled in the wind. According to the stories we heard, these spirits came from water bodies and traveled in the wind, looking for a place to settle and people to possess. To avoid having them settle in your home, one had to make a lot of noise and hit metallic objects to scare them away whenever they were passing by.

Sometimes the *nyawawa* made their trip earlier in the night before we fell asleep. Our cue was usually the noise and screams from the villages surrounding the school. They would shout, "Nyawawa! Nyawawa!" while hitting *sufurias,* and we would quickly reach for spoons, metal cups and plates, and whatever else we could find that was metallic, and make as much noise as we could. Some of the girls thought it was fun, but to me, it was terrifying, especially when it happened in the middle of the night when everyone was asleep.

Most of the time nobody woke up to hit things and make noise if the *nyawawa* passed by late at night. The villagers would do their usual thing, but the dorms remained quiet. Sometimes one could hear the wind outside, and it was said that if you listened carefully enough, you would hear the *nyawawa* speaking in the wind. I was crippled with fear at the thought of being possessed. And so unless I was with my cousin, I would quietly slip out of my bunk bed and get into my school mother's bed below me.

At the end of that first year, Sheila graduated from high school. My father did not think I was ready to remain in that school without someone to take care of me. He was right. I was slightly more independent, but living in that school was like being in a horror movie. With my cousin gone, and my school mother possibly leaving as well if she ended up placed at a different high school, I would definitely struggle to survive in that environment.

Lucky for me, I did not have to explain any of that to my father. He already knew I needed a different environment, and so he transferred me to a different boarding school where my other cousin, Sheila's younger sister, was.

The new school was a slight improvement of the previous one.

There was more structure and more adult presence. Unlike the previous school, the adults in this school actually cared to know what was happening with the students. They would notice if someone failed to show up for a meal. They even went as far as having some of the junior nuns sleep in our dorms.

I felt safer there. We got beaten more often at the new school, but at least there were no ghosts, and no *nyawawa*. The convent was only a few meters from the dorms, and the nuns were always around. Right across the fence was a boys high school, and Sheila's brother went to school there. I rarely saw or talked to him, but just knowing that he was there was a bit of a comfort.

Unlike Sheila and her other siblings, the cousin that I found in that school was heartless. She was aggressive, loud, and did not seem to have a caring bone in her body. I had previously never interacted closely with her even though our families were close. She actively ignored me every time we met, and being a more laid back personality, I never tried to make friends with her. Her energy was too overwhelming for me.

This cousin was rough in her interactions with me. I was never sure if she liked me or hated me, if she was complimenting me or insulting me. I had been excited to join her at the school, hoping that since we were closer in age, we would be friends. But soon enough, I discovered that there was no possibility I could have any kind of positive relationship with this girl. She started spreading rumors about my family. She had a lot to share, considering how close our families were, and she was quite generous with the stories. Her own friends would turn around and tell me everything, and there was no doubt the stories were coming from her because nobody else in that school knew my family in such intimate detail. It hurt to hear those stories, but I chose to ignore and stay away from her.

One time, her father came to visit, and being my uncle, he asked if I needed anything. I requested him to tell my father that I needed a new bucket. Mr. Maina decided to buy me a bucket from the nearby shopping center rather than bother my father about something so small. But the moment he left, my cousin grabbed the bucket from me saying it belonged to her since it was her father who bought it.

I wrote my father a long, tearful letter explaining the difficulty I was having with my cousin. As soon as my father received the letter, he traveled to the school, brought me a bucket, and told me not to pay attention to the girl. She was just being a child, he said. But my problems with my cousin did not end there. We stopped talking to each other altogether. One day, she got some bread from her brother across the fence and gave some to one of her friends to bring to me. Bread was a major treat because it was considered contraband, and we basically never saw a slice of bread served in that school. Those with connections across the fence were able to sneak a loaf here and there, but for those of us with neither the connections nor the guts to befriend boys on the other side, we could only dream of this delicacy.

This girl knew that I would be tempted to accept her bread

even though we weren't talking to each other. Maybe it was a peace offering, or maybe it was a trap to get me indebted to her somehow. Either way, I was so deeply hurt by everything she had done to me since I joined the school that even the offer of bread was not enough to make me want anything to do with her. I politely declined the bread.

When the bread was taken back to her, she got wildly angry and came over to confront me. We got into an argument and exchanged some words. She came at me and was ready to start a physical fight, but was quickly restrained by other students. I did not speak to her again for many years after that.

The fall out with my cousin woke me up to the reality that I was truly on my own at the boarding school. I functioned decently without support. I could wash my own clothes, and as long as I had that covered, everything else was routine. There was no family system in that school, no school mothers or sisters to help one settle in. The nuns were always around, but they were harsh and quite heavy handed. The teachers flogged us like horses. We got beaten for any reason, including answering questions incorrectly in exams, talking in class, being late for anything, and so on. The world in that little Catholic school was a cold cold place.

Running Away

I braved through the months in boarding school, keeping a low profile and trying hard not to cause any trouble. But almost every term, the moment schools closed and I got home, I immediately fell sick. My father would get very concerned about me. The sickness was like my body's way of releasing the built up tension of school, and it certainly got a lot of my father's attention. I enjoyed my father's gentleness and care, which was something none of my siblings seemed to ever get from him. It felt good to be treated like a favorite child.

We moved from the rented two story house to an even larger bungalow that my father built. It was a humongous six bedroom, five bath house with a large compound, and an even larger adjoining piece of land where my father built some shops, a posho mill, and some rental property. By the standards of the area, we were officially rich.

In addition to his insurance brokers business, his real estate business, and a number of other smaller businesses he had, my father got into the transport business. He bought two mini buses that ran the Kisumu-Kisii route. This significantly increased the number of relatives that came to visit us, because all they had to do was show up at the Kisii bus stop, narrate the great relationship that they had with my father, and get a free ride to Kisumu.

Mama, my father was a terrible husband to you, and a way less than perfect father to us, but one thing I can proudly say about him is that he was industrious, and successful in his businesses. He was a self made man that used his God-given smarts and personality to advance himself and create wealth at a young age.

To me, my father seemed self-assured, like he knew everything about everything. I admired him and feared him in equal measure.

While the year we moved in with him my father had spent a lot of time out with friends, he stayed home more often now. He stopped smoking, which was surprising because previously, my father could barely make it one hour without lighting a cigarette.

He smoked whole packets of cigarettes per day. I had come to love the smell of cigarette smoke. It was the smell I most closely associated with my father, and although he inspired a lot of fear and anxiety in me, having the smell of my father around our house was something that I cherished.

Once the cigarettes were gone, and my father was spending a lot more time at home, I started to notice some changes in him. He coughed a lot. He also got angry a lot faster than was usual for him. Most of his anger was directed at my brothers since they were more likely to be in close proximity to him than my sisters and I. We, the girls, stayed either in our bedroom, or in the kitchen most of the time. I was very quiet and nice around my father, and I had learned to be very careful not to give him reason to get upset with me.

My father got more and more paranoid by the day. He accused us of a number of things, including stealing from him. He didn't point to anyone specifically, but for days, he went around the house saying that we were stealing things from him. We all remained quiet and did not try to defend ourselves any time he started with the accusations. He was not entirely wrong about the stealing. He always left his room open, and because he was not very careful with his money, we all sometimes did grab a coin here and there. Personally, I would grab at most five shillings at a time to buy a treat. I think my brothers took larger amounts of money. Enough that my father would notice.

Whenever he came home, we would all scatter to our rooms or to the kitchen to minimize our interaction with him as much as possible. The more we avoided him, the more paranoid he became about our activities. He would leave the house, pretending to go to work, then park his car somewhere and sneak back home, maybe hoping to catch us in the act of stealing from him, or whatever else he thought we were up to.

On the Christmas eve of the year after your passing, my father came home unexpectedly in the middle of the day. He looked particularly agitated. He announced that he was going to conduct an impromptu search of our rooms.

The boys were first. All three of them were summoned and taken to their rooms. My oldest brother had his own room while the younger two shared a room. He started with the younger boys' room. They opened their suitcases, flipped over mattresses, and turned the room upside down at his command. Nothing. They then proceeded to my older brother's room. My father searched every nook and crook. When he couldn't find anything, he grabbed a bible that was on the desk and angrily hit my brother with it. He then proceeded to grab him and start beating him up.

My sisters and I were in the kitchen. We were cowering with fear, wondering what was happening in our brothers' rooms. We locked the kitchen door when we heard screams. Mama, it was like when I was four years old all over again. In my mind, the only thing I could think about was death. I feared my father was going to kill my brothers.

After a few minutes of screaming, we heard running, and when we looked out the kitchen window, saw our brothers taking off towards the gate.

My father came banging on the kitchen door and demanding that we open up. My sister opened the door.

It was time to search our room. My father ordered my sisters to go open up their suitcases. He said I was fine. I didn't need to come for the search. So I stayed in the kitchen as my sisters were ushered to the bedroom we all shared for inspection. While the house had many bedrooms, all three of us girls ended up sharing a room, and a bed. I was never sure why since even the house girl had a room of her own. But I was used to sharing a room with my sisters, and so I did not question it.

My father accused my sisters of stealing your stuff, including your clothes and some fabric that you left behind. He was not entirely wrong. Except for the use of the word stealing. My sisters did take some of your clothes from my father's room, not to wear them because I don't believe your style matched theirs. It was probably more sentimental than anything else.

When asked to open the trunk that they had kept those clothes in, my sisters said the key was lost. So my father went outside, got a machete, and cut the trunk open. He found your old clothes and some of your fabric in there, thus confirming his theory that we were stealing from him.

Mama, I don't know why my father was concerned about your clothes and your fabric. I don't think there was much he could do with them. Did he miss you, maybe? Was he finally coming back to his senses and realizing how horribly he had treated you?

I sat in the kitchen, the all too familiar feeling of pain in my chest being a constant companion. Because of the chaos of the day, we did not cook lunch that day. But I was not hungry at all. I was too scared to even think about eating.

My father ordered my sisters to take everything from our room and our brothers' rooms and put them in a pile outside. They carried everything out, including mattresses. The only things that were left in the bedrooms were the beds and the cupboards.

"Mami!" My father called.
I jumped, my chest pumping uncontrollably. I felt like an animal whose time to go to the slaughter house had come. When I got outside, my father told me to pick everything of mine out of the pile outside.

"You are a good girl." He said. "You are the only one that doesn't steal from me, the only good child that I have."

I picked out my clothes from the pile, sneaking in some of my sisters' clothes as well. My father said he was going to burn everything that was left in that pile. He was going to burn everything that belonged to anyone in that house except his stuff and my stuff. I was flattered that my father was upset with everyone but me. But I was also extremely afraid.

When my father went into the house to get matchsticks and some gasoline, Lena said we had to run.
"He could kill us if we stay," she said.
It was not even a debate. Bonareri said she was going. And of course I was going with my sisters. There was no way I was going to be left alone with my father. It didn't matter that he said I was a good child. If it came down to it, and I was the only one available for him to take his anger out on, I believed my father could seriously harm me.

And so we took off- out the gate, through some bushy paths, through other people's compounds, and out into an unfamiliar world. We had no idea where we were going.

Mama, I have had many nightmares over the years of this run away from home experience. In my nightmares, I am usually out of breath, running through the same bushes, through strangers' homes, while someone evil is hot on my heels, closing in on me. Even as an adult, I still have this nightmare every now and then.

We ran for a long time. Night fell. We were still unsure about where we were and where we were going. I was scared. But I was less scared out there than I would have been had I stayed alone with my father. Even as I doubted the wisdom of my sister's decision, I was still confident that following her was better than risking my father's wrath by staying home.

Just as my panic was setting in, we found ourselves on a main road. Finally we had a sense of where we were. With Lena leading us, we walked along the road until we started to see buildings that were familiar. We were at the town center.

Lena said she could find the way to our old neighborhood from there. It was a long way from the town center, but we did not have any money to take a *matatu*.

As we were walking across town, we saw our father's car slowly drive by. He seemed to be driving around aimlessly, maybe looking for us. We quickly turned away from the road so he wouldn't see us. I was exhausted. I wanted to shout for him to come and get us, but my fear of him at that moment was greater than my desire to rest my feet. And so we watched him drive away, and continued on our way on foot.

Lena was able to get us to our old neighborhood. Luckily, my friend Peace's mother was home. Peace and the rest of the family had traveled upcountry for Christmas, but her mother and their housegirl were there. She took us in, offered us dinner, and gave us a place to sleep. I hadn't eaten anything since breakfast that day, but I could not eat. I was unable to even attempt putting anything in my mouth that night. My chest hurt, my stomach hurt, my feet hurt. I felt like I could throw up. I had just walked a distance longer than I could have imagined possible. Most of my pain though was confined to the chest and stomach, and it was more anxiety pain than pain from the actual running and walking.

The next morning, we woke up early, and graciously accepted Mama Peace's offer of a warm shower and breakfast. I missed Peace, but I was too full of survival adrenalin to think much about her that day. Her mother saw us off, and we continued on our way.

Lena knew the way to Mr. Maina, my father's best friend's house. It was Christmas morning. When we got there, they were just getting ready to leave the house. They were going to spend Christmas with another family. My sister told my uncle what had transpired at home. He had us change into our cousins' clothes, and join them for Christmas at their family friend's house.

It was an awkward Christmas. We did not know the family at whose house we were spending the day. So we sat awkwardly in their living room, ate nice food, watched television, and tried to take up as little space as possible.

At the end of the day, my uncle said he was taking us back home. We protested, citing my father's anger, and the possibility that he could hurt us. My uncle promised us that none of that was going to happen. That he would talk to our father and calm him down.

When we got home, our brothers were already back. My father said nothing to us. He spoke to uncle Maina and then went to his room for the night. Our stuff was still outside. We took a few things back inside, so we could have somewhere to sleep for the night. We traded stories in hushed voices. The boys said they had run to the house of our former houseboy, who was now an administrative assistant at my father's office. They spent the night, and came back home with their host in the morning. The young man had the same serious, perfectly chiseled face, but was more polished and looked very much the part as a newly promoted Administrative Assistant.

My father had made the boys sit outside in the sun all day despite pleas from his Assistant to let them in the house. The boys had to sit on some stones under the scorching sun while my father went about his day, completely ignoring them.
My father didn't speak to us at all for days. He seemed genuinely hurt, and that was confusing to me because what did he expect would happen after threatening to beat people up and burn everything down? He didn't personally threaten me, but even I would not have waited around to find out what he was capable of doing.

When he finally did speak to us, it was both terrifying, and a great relief. My brothers and I were eating quietly at the dinner table. My father came and joined us. My sisters were in the kitchen, where they ate most of their meals. He was silent for a while, then loudly banged his fist on the table.

My heart jumped and started racing in panic.
"I have never seen such ungrateful children." He said.
He went into a rant about everything that he had done for us, and how we chose to repay him with such behavior as we had displayed when we all ran away from home.
"I was going to buy you things for Christmas!" He said. "But do I even have children I can spend money on? What kind of children are these?"

He was clearly hurt by our running away. And hurt was never a feeling I had imagined my father capable of. We listened quietly, not daring to look him in the eye. I was afraid he would get violent again. I was sitting right next to him, and in my mind, I was calculating the best escape route should things get ugly.
"And you!" He turned to yell at me. "Where were *you* trying to go?"
I lowered my eyes and said nothing.
"Why were you running? What did you think I was going to do to you?"

I could not speak. I kept my eyes on the ground. Briefly, I considered the possibility that I might have made a mistake by following my sisters when they decided to run away. I could see that my father was disappointed in my choice, and he was hurt by it. But deep down, I kept going back to the violence I knew he was capable of. I could not trust my father enough to be left alone with him when he was angry.

After the rant at the dinner table, my father never brought up the incident again. He did not beat anyone up or burn anything. We took our stuff back into our rooms and quietly moved on as though nothing had happened.

Men on the Walls

My father's illness crept in over a period of time. I could see changes in him, but I didn't really know he was sick until he started to bring witch doctors to the house. One witch doctor told us there was a lot of bad medicine buried all over our compound. He said somebody really wanted us dead. So to counter the strength of the bad medicine, he slaughtered some animals, spilled their blood around the outside of our house and buried the carcasses at various spots where he felt the bad medicine was particularly strong. He also said some trees we had planted in the compound were bad omen. That when their roots reached the house, someone in the family would die.

I did not exactly judge what my father was doing, but I struggled to understand why he believed in witch doctors. He was one of the sons in his family that seemed to be more like his mother. My family was Catholic, including my father, and I had taken catechism classes, was baptized and confirmed in the Catholic church. I did not believe in witchcraft. But I had a lot of love and admiration for my father, even when I saw him walking around the house with the blood of a dead chicken in the hopes that it would cure him of whatever ailment he had.

My father used to visit me almost every other week when I first went to boarding school. These visits became further and further apart as he continued to get ill. I got used to not seeing him. I also isolated myself more and more from other people. I was neither sad nor happy. I was simply existing through the days, not thinking about anything, not feeling anything. I did what was expected of me and got lost in the sea of other girls.

One day my father came to visit me at school. He had hired a driver since he could no longer drive himself. He put his feet on the grass outside of the car, but could not stand up. I did not even realize that the reason he did not fully get out of the car was that he was too weak to pull himself up. To me, he looked fine. He had lost a lot of weight, but in my eyes, he still looked okay. Or maybe I was in denial.

I stood next to him as he sat in the car. He asked about school, if I was doing okay, if I was working hard. I was neither okay nor working hard, but I said yes to both. I wasn't exactly badly off either. I was numb. I was surviving.

That was the last time my father came to the school. On the last day of that term, we had a parent's day. My father did not show up. I was not surprised. I was not upset either. When I went to the school in Busia, we had many parents events that you never showed up to even though our house was practically next door to the school. How could I then begrudge my father not coming to a parent's day at a school that was miles away from home? I learned to make my own way home by taking the school's hired public transport that went all the way to Kisumu town. I would then take a taxi home from there.

Mama, if my father neglected and hurt you at your most vulnerable, when you were on your deathbed, then he got a good dose of his own medicine when he got sick. He became a completely different man; a far cry from the rich, popular businessman that he was just a few months prior. He used to have a beehive of friends, spent just about every evening in bars, entertaining people with free drinks, and only came home in the wee hours of the morning. My father even paid a musician to compose a song about him. Granted, it was a song aimed at promoting his insurance business, but the song praised him a lot, as a person. At some point, he even tried to run for mayor, though that plan fell through in the early stages.

All those friends disappeared when he got sick. Not even his family came to see him anymore.

Mama, my father became a lot like you as he continued to deteriorate. He became irritable, angry all the time. He would refuse to eat unless the food was prepared exactly the way he wanted it. He was often nauseous, and sometimes the only thing he could eat was sugar free tea biscuits. One time Lena made some rice and beef stew and took it to his room. She had been away at college and was unaware that he was too sick to eat meat. My father took the plate of food and threw it in her face.

There were rumors that my father had AIDS. I did not believe them. In my mind, AIDS was not something anyone in my family could have, and especially not my father. I was more likely at that point to believe that my father was bewitched than I was to believe that he had AIDS. I already knew that a lot of people did not like our family, including relatives, because my father was quite successful as a businessman. And so I took anything I heard about us with a grain of salt.

Mama, the path towards death is a painful and lonely one. My father was in a humiliating state. I saw you sick, but either I was too young and separated from you to comprehend the extent of your illness, or your illness did not hit you as strongly as my father's hit him. He started to have hallucinations. At the time, I didn't understand that it was his fever and illness that was making him see things. I believed that he was actually seeing the things that he said he saw.

According to my father, someone had put bad medicine in his bedroom. He kept saying that those relatives who used to come to our house had sneaked into his room and performed some witchcraft there. When he lay on his bed, he saw men on the walls, and they talked to him, terrorizing him, threatening him. The men were his ancestors. They were there for his life, to take him away to the cold and dreary land of the dead.

He brought his mattress and bedding out into the living room to escape the torture of the men on the walls. My brothers and I also brought our bedding, and we all slept together on the living room floor.

My father made the same kind of sounds in his throat that you did when you were sick. It was like an audible shiver. Like he was very cold inside, and the internal chill was coming out through his throat. The sound was familiar in a way that made my heart pound and my stomach ache.

Another One of Us Falls

Despite knowing that my father was very sick, somehow I still expected that he would come pick me up from school at the end of the next term. I was eleven years old and in grade six. Nobody had visited me at all that term. I did not think much of it. In fact, I spent very little time thinking about my father. Most of my time at school was spent trying to survive and avoid getting in trouble.

Since he did not send any money for my transport though, I expected that my father was coming for me. I got myself ready and waited, not at all worried. However, when afternoon came and he hadn't shown up yet, I started to wonder if he even knew it was closing day. I'd written him a letter about it weeks before, but never received a response. I wondered if he had missed it.

Just when I was about to lose hope, I saw a Wonder Tree minibus coming through the school gate. My father had added several vehicles to his fleet, and seeing one of them at school gave me such pride. I got my bags, signed myself out, and ran to it.

My father's younger brother was on the minibus, along with the driver, and a few other men I did not know. He took my bags, told me to find a seat, and yelled for the driver to go. I gathered that they had gone on their usual routes before coming for me, and even as we drove home, they picked some passengers along the way. I did not care. I was happy to sit quietly in my window seat and let my mind wander off.

My grandmother greeted me at the door when we got home. She was overwhelmingly affectionate, but it felt good to be hugged after enduring months at the boarding school without seeing anyone from home. She said my father was very sick. One of his brothers, who was staying at our house at the time, would take me to see him at the hospital in the morning.

I listened to my grandmother pray late into the night. It was like a chant: the same words over and over again as she recited the rosary. I did not think or feel anything about my father being at the hospital. I recognized it as a fact, but felt nothing about it. My mind was closed off to anything other than what was right in front of me. I lay in my bed with my eyes closed, allowing myself to be comforted by the sound of my grandmother's prayers. Soon I was fast asleep.

The drive to the hospital was long and lonely. I did not have anything to say to my uncle, and he did not seem to have anything to say to me either. So we drove in silence. I stared aimlessly out the window, and in the background, some old school music played.

The hospital was located in a small town with most of its activities concentrated in one area. There were shops, kiosks, women selling fruits and vegetables by the roadside. I stared at them through the car window and wondered what their lives were like. I wondered where they lived, if they had any children. As we pulled into the hospital compound, I wondered if my father would be happy to see me.

Seeing my father on the hospital bed was a shock. I had expected that he would look weak, but what I saw was unlike anything I had ever seen in my life. My father was gone, and all there was on that bed was a skeleton with the skin still on it.

The shock must have been evident all over my face. I froze at the door for a few seconds.

This was the private wing of the wards, so my father had an ensuite room all to himself. I stared, unable to decide what to do with myself.

"Mami," he said.

I walked over and sat next to him on the bed. He reached out and touched my arm. I moved closer. His eyes were like big bulbs protruding out of a sunken face. This great man that was once a young and vibrant big shot, the man that occupied space like a boss, rolling in money, with expensive taste, had been reduced to looking like a famine stricken child.

He asked about school, like he always did. Asked if I had a good term, if I did well in my exams. My father is the only person in my family that ever showed concern for my grades. I told him that I did well, even though I didn't. He reiterated that I was a good girl, and that he was happy with me. My father always told me that I was good, and so I strived to live up to that expectation for him.

Watching him struggle to speak was painful. My chest hurt. The man in front of me was skin and bones, with not an ounce of flesh on him. His face was sunken, and the outlines of his bones visible through his skin. Very badly I wanted to cry. But I could not. My eyes were as dry as they had ever been, and they just would not get in sync with what my mind told me I should do.

My father fell asleep soon after. He kept making those shivering noises. My uncle and I sat quietly by his side all day. At one point, he woke up and attempted to get out of bed. My uncle tried to help him up but he angrily pushed him away. He seemed to be in a hurry. And maybe he did not want me to see him needing help to get up.

He painfully pulled himself up and waddled across the small room, trying to get to the toilet. Before he could get there, his bladder gave way and the urine came running down his legs and onto the floor. My uncle rushed to his side and helped him the few remaining steps to the toilet. I got up immediately and walked out of the room.

I knew I was not supposed to have seen that, and I could sense my father's shame at his own helplessness. I felt shame for him, and for myself after having seen him like that.

I didn't know where to go when I left the room. The hospital smelled strongly of disinfectant, and for some reason, that smell made me nervous. I walked aimlessly outside for a while before coming back into the ward. My father was asleep. I sat on his bed and just watched him breathe. I was sad for him, and my chest hurt from the awareness that my father was dying. But my heart refused to process that reality. I could clearly see what was in front of me, my mind could process it as fact, but my heart was not open to letting it sink. I remember just sitting there watching my father sleep, and thinking, well, this is my reality now. This is where we are. And that was that.

When we got back home in the evening, we found my three brothers at home. Their schools had just closed. We did not talk about our father. They knew that I had just come from visiting him, but they asked me nothing, and I volunteered no information either. I imagine we all knew what was happening, and nobody wanted to talk about it. There was really nothing to say.
The next day, we all traveled with my uncle back to the hospital. I was glad that I got to see my father again.

He looked just as weak as he had been the previous day. My

uncle propped him up so he could try and eat. He tried one spoonful of his food and pushed it away. His brother tried to beg him to eat, but he got angry and said something mean in Kisii. My father was gentle with us, but seemed highly irritable with his brother. He completely refused to eat the food, and instead told us to eat it. We were hungry, so we ate without giving it a second thought, unaware that in my uncle's eyes, we had just committed an unforgivable crime by eating a sick person's food.

Later, my father sent my uncle away so that he could talk to us.

"I'm dying," he said. "I can feel it. I know that I don't have much longer to live."
None of us said anything. We sat there helplessly, watching him struggle to talk.
"But I am fighting," he said. "I will fight to the very last minute."

We listened quietly. It felt like there was nothing to say. Our relationship with our father was not exactly one that invited a lot of conversation. Usually, he talked, we listened, and only spoke when required to do so.

"You will be fine," he said. "You are old enough to take care of yourselves. And I have left you enough money to help you."

He went on to tell us that we should never trust anyone that claims they can take care of us, and especially not our uncles. He was confident that we could make it on our own. It is better to stay on your own than to stay with these people, he said.

"They will take everything from you. I know that is what they are waiting for. Do not let them lie to you that they are going to take care of you."

My father outlined the property that he had and to whom he had left each piece. He spoke of the real estate, and if he mentioned anything else, I must not have understood what he was talking about. All I remember hearing was that the various properties had been left to my three brothers. My name did not appear anywhere in the conversation about property. It was as though I had disappeared from the room. I was only eleven years old, but I remember feeling invisible, like I did not matter. I felt as though I was not as much my father's child as my brothers were. It was not about the property, because at that age my father's wealth meant nothing to me personally. It was more about belonging, and being in a room where my presence was totally overlooked.

The exclusion made me disconnect from the situation even more. I was there, but I felt as though none of what was happening had anything to do with me. My father's fondness of me suddenly felt fake and meaningless.
We got back home to Kisumu late at night. I went straight to bed.

We were never allowed to go visit my father at the hospital again after that. My uncle said it was because the last time we were there, we ate my father's food. We promised never to eat hospital food again, but my uncle would not hear it. My oldest brother, Paul, who was in high school at the time, went to stay at the hospital as my father's caregiver, but my uncle completely refused to let the rest of us see our father again.

About a week later, three of my father's other brothers and our grandfather all showed up at our house on the same day. Two of his brothers and our grandmother were already with us, so when this next group showed up, it became a full house. There was a certain energy to my father's family that was both exciting and frightening. Exciting because they all had massive personalities and were sure to have something going that would add spice to the days, and frightening because they were equally capable of just as much violence and chaos as my father was.

They were nice to us, but they seemed to have their agenda set out and were busy focusing on that. The family spent a lot of time in a house that was right next to the main house. My father had built it as a guest house, but it was mostly unutilized. The brothers and their parents gathered in that house every night for what seemed like secret meetings. We were not invited, and neither were we told what the purpose of those meetings was. But we could speculate. My father had told us not to trust his family, and so I imagined that those meetings were part of the reason why. We tried to sneak up to the guest house and eavesdrop at the window, but we could not make out what they were saying.

My father's sisters were conspicuously missing from these family meetings. It seemed as though the girls in that family did not matter at all. Once they were out of their mother's house, they were as good as forgotten. I wondered if anyone had even told them that their brother was dying. The brothers and their parents would spend the days at the hospital with my father, never allowing us to come along, and then they would gather in the guest house at night, behind closed doors, and have discussions for hours.

During my father's illness, and generally in his last year of life, the only friend that stuck with him was a newer one that we called Uncle Philip. Even his best friend, Uncle Maina, abandoned him when death came knocking. He suddenly just stopped showing up, and his wife and children also disappeared from our lives. The only one I saw sometimes was the one at my school, but I never spoke to her at all. As fate would have it, she and I ended up getting admission to the same high school two years apart. She was two years ahead of me, so by the time I joined, she was in form three. But our relationship was already damaged beyond repair. Just like our fathers' relationship.

Uncle Philip spent a lot of time at our house. He became the only adult that I trusted in the whole confusion of everything that was happening in our lives. As my father's family stuck around, acting weird, Uncle Philip would stop by almost every day to check on us and ensure we were not starving. He would bring us groceries, spend time chatting with us and cheering us up. To me, he was the best thing that had happened to our family in a while. He was warm, genuinely kind, and his presence made me feel safe. I knew that my father trusted him, and so I trusted him. He was a tall, lean, athletic man with quick strides when he walked, and a permanent smile on his face. He wasn't a blood relative as far as I knew, but he was the only person my father had indicated to us was truly on our side.

I had a lot of time to prepare for my father's death. We all knew it was coming. I rehearsed my reaction to the news. I hoped I would have some tears, although that seemed unlikely, considering I had had none for you when you died, and none yet for my father, even though he had already told us himself that he was dying. I still hoped though that I would be able to have some kind of appropriate reaction.

It was immediately obvious to me what had happened when one afternoon, the brothers and their parents pulled up in a Wonder Tree van, faces heavy, and my grandmother started wailing while calling out my father's name. My heart jumped and that familiar pain in my chest reawakened with intensity. I was sitting outside. I immediately got up and ran into the bedroom I shared with my sisters. As much as I had prepared myself for this day, I was caught off guard and I didn't immediately know what to do. Running seemed like my only option at the time.

I sat quietly on the bed, my heart racing. In my mind, I was thinking that this was it, the moment had come. I willed myself to conjure up the appropriate reaction. But there was no appropriate reaction. I didn't have any tears. I had rehearsed so much for this moment, but I could not get myself to do anything other than sit there quietly, my chest thumping, listening to my grandmother's wailing.

My grandmother walked around the compound sobbing and chanting about her son. She was holding the small radio that my father had in his hospital room, and his walking stick. I stayed in the bedroom and did not talk to anyone until I heard Uncle Philip's voice. I came out and went to him. He put an arm around me and said he was very sorry about my father. He asked if we had eaten. I said yes. He sat with me in the living room for a bit, then went into my father's bedroom. Uncle Philip had free access to my father's room since he spent a lot of time there when my father was sick. He locked himself in my father's room and broke into loud sobs. That took me by surprise. I had never heard a man cry so shamelessly. My father's own brothers did not shed a tear as far as I could tell, but Uncle Philip let it all out. He sobbed and sobbed, and as much as I hated hearing people cry, I thought his reaction was beautiful. It did not irritate me the way other people's cries irritated me. Uncle Philip's crying confirmed to me that he did indeed care about my father. I wondered if he would adopt me, make me his daughter, now that both you and my father were dead.

The Last Matchstick

We were informed of a plan to split the six of us between my father's six brothers. The six brothers would then split my father's assets so that each of them got an equal share to help them support the child they took. One of my uncles actually told me about this plan the very same day that my father died. It was his own weird way of assuring me that they had a plan for our care in the absence of my father. My sisters and I later laughed about this suggestion. What my uncles did not know was that my father had already thought through everything that could happen with his family after his death.

The atmosphere surrounding my father's death day was very different from yours. Rather than real mourners, I felt like we were surrounded by vultures, and that there was a storm brewing somewhere in the background, waiting for the opportune time to land. None of us kids were in tears. In fact, the very next day after my father died, I was outside singing and dancing as my siblings watched. My brother reminded me about this for years. He'd gone back to school for holiday tuition since he was in grade seven, and so after my father died, one of my uncles went to the school to get him. He walked through the gate expecting to find people crying. Instead, he was greeted by the sight of me dancing and singing out loud in front of our house. It was not that I was not saddened by my father's passing. I just couldn't bring myself to cry. And I realized later in life that sometimes I made a lot of noise, probably as a coping mechanism, when my mind was in distress.

The storm did finally land. Our house was full of relatives. The brothers' wives and their children had joined, and my father's sisters, and your sisters, and many of their children. I was excited to have so many cousins my age around. We played all day while the women cooked and cleaned and the men held meetings. We heard rumors about how the brothers were plotting to split my father's assets. We said nothing. Our opinion was never sought.

One night, as we sat around the living room with cousins and our aunts, we heard commotion and shouts coming from outside. Two of the brothers were fighting. We all ran outside, but by the time we got there, both brothers had already fled. There was blood on the ground. Turned out, the fight had resulted in one brother biting off a slice of the upper lip of the other. He bit his brother's lip all the way off. Prior to this incident, years prior, another brother had bitten off a slice of his brother's ear. It was almost hilarious. The family seemed to have very sharp teeth, and they weren't shy about using them to bite off flesh from each other's body parts.

A younger brother had to separate the lip-biting fight with a machete. He showed up and started slapping them with the flat side of the machete, prompting them both to get up and take off into the night.

The story we heard later was that the two brothers had disagreed on asset distribution following my father's death, and they decided to settle it physically. As this story was being narrated soon after the scuffle ended and the brothers took off, their wives were crying hysterically. One of them was your former student that you had introduced to your brother-in-law. She kept crying while calling out your name and asking what kind of family you had brought her into.

The two men showed back up the next day. The one with the cut lip had gone to hospital and seemed to have some stitches. But a chunk of his upper lip was missing.

It rained heavily the day my father's body was brought home from the mortuary. Our house was full to the brim with friends and relatives we hadn't seen in a long time. Mrs. Maina was walking around the house giving instructions to everyone as though she was the hostess. She and her husband had disappeared from our lives throughout my father's illness. I found a seat at a corner in the living room and stayed in one spot. That way I could avoid attracting attention and minimize my chances of having to talk to anyone.

My father's casket was on a table in the middle of the living room. I wanted to walk over and take a look inside, but there were too many people around. I was afraid they would be watching me for a reaction. And I didn't think I would have the kind of reaction they might expect. I wasn't going to cry. Everything that was happening around me seemed removed from me as a person. It was as though it was not my problem. There was nothing in me that was overly devastated.

It did not seem like the number of people in the house was going to reduce any time soon, so eventually I gathered up the courage and walked over to the casket to view my father's body. I was slightly nervous, mostly because I knew people were watching me. But I really wanted to see my father's body.

He looked better in death than he did in his last days of life. His face was fuller, and he fit beautifully in his suit. It seemed as though they had stuffed some flesh back in him, or pumped him up full of something, because he was definitely not the bag of bones I had seen a few weeks prior. I wondered why they hadn't done the same for you two years before, because when I viewed your body, it was thin, dry, and wrinkled, and it looked nothing like you. My father's body looked more like the body of a real person.

After viewing the body, I walked out of the room. Mrs. Maina followed me into the kitchen and pulled me in for a hug. I let her hug me for as long as she needed to, and when she finally let me go, I walked away without a word.

The next morning, we traveled to our rural home in Kisii. This time it was like "take two" of the same movie scene. The convoy of cars, the mourners staring through the windows, women wailing, men walking around the compound looking busy, children mesmerized. I was less disturbed by the mourners this time. My father's sisters went around the compound wailing, even though they were never that close to him. They had a decent sibling relationship, but none of them was a regular presence in our lives. Mourning their brother was an expectation, and they dutifully complied.

We woke up bright and early on the day of his burial ceremony. I had never seen so many people in my life. My sisters and I had on matching black and white skirts and white blouses, while the boys had matching suits. We sat in the front row, facing the casket. I have no recollection of a single thing that was said or done at that ceremony. Similar to your burial, I was not invited to the graveside for the lowering of the casket. That honor was reserved for the sons. My mind wandered off the entire time, and the next thing I knew, my father was already buried and everyone was leaving.

The women of the home were expected to clean up that evening. Apparently, it was an important expectation, because when the wife of one of my father's brothers failed to show up for the cleaning, the other women went to her house, dragged her out and publicly flogged her.

I must have been numb to everything, because even as this was happening, I was neither scared nor entertained. I watched the events unfold as though they were normal. My uncle, the woman's husband, was informed that his wife was being flogged. He came running with a big stick, mercilessly whipped whoever he could find while all the women scattered in different directions. My uncle then went around the compound yelling and swearing to kill someone if they ever lay a hand on his wife again. It was quite ironic because this was the same uncle that beat all his wives to near death at the slightest provocation.

That night, the men drank themselves silly. My younger brother, then around ten years old, was handed a drink as well, and the men entertained themselves by pushing him to drink up. By the time my brother was getting back to the house, he could barely walk. He was staggering and laughing like a crazy person. There was nothing any of us could do about it. He slept it off, and everyone pretended like it never happened.

In the next few days, I spent time exploring the farm and the river with my cousins. Family meetings were ongoing, but I was never invited to any of them. My sister Lena told me that they wanted us to stay there permanently. My father's family already had a plan for what the rest of our lives were going to look like. It was expected that my two sisters would get married soon, and that my brothers and I would stay in Kisii with our grandmother.

This was not presented as a suggestion, or a request, but rather as a decision. I'm not sure at what point my uncles found out that grabbing my father's assets was not going to be that easy. My father had already transferred most of his property to my brothers, and there was no legal way they could get their hands on it. Once they found this out, they became hostile and the insults started flying in. One of my uncles said that even if we went back to our house in Kisumu, we would not find anything there because they were going to take everything, down to the last matchstick. He said that we would end up becoming *chokoraas*, begging on the streets, and we would go back to them begging for help.

Lena had a good sense of humor about the whole thing, and I think that helped me not to take any of it too seriously. We laughed about it and imagined what the life they had planned for us would have looked like, living in rural Kisii, in a mud hut, going to local schools, after coming from a six-bedroomed bungalow in a relatively big town and from fairly good boarding schools.

We stayed in Kisii for what seemed like a long time. I was not fully aware of what was going on, but there were rumors that my uncles had vowed not to let us leave. Despite these rumors, I was not worried. I was at a place emotionally where nothing was really sinking in. Even if we had been sold off in an auction at that point in my life, I would probably still not have been worried.

One morning, my siblings and I were outside playing when we saw a small convoy of police cars driving into the compound. Every adult in the vicinity disappeared in a flash. All anyone in that compound had to hear was the word police, and they would break their legs jumping over fences to get away.

I saw my uncle Philip come out of one of the cars, a towering presence, tall, confident, and full of life. I idolized him. I could almost say I had a dad crush on him. I wanted so badly for him to adopt me and be my new father.

Uncle Philip looked out for us in many ways after our father's death. He brought the police all the way to my father's rural home to ensure we were able to get out of there safely. After we'd packed our stuff and gotten out of there under police escort, Uncle Philip traveled with us back to Kisumu, ensured that we settled back into our house, and checked in on us from time to time. He was just about the only friend of my father's that stuck with us through the desperation of the years that followed.

CHAPTER FOUR

Dear Mama,

I was quite numb and oblivious to what was going on around me. My uncles and my grandmother were fighting with each other, and with my sister, Lena. My father's sisters disappeared from our lives as soon as the funeral was over. Even at the funeral itself, they were barely present. They made an appearance, did not exert themselves, and said nothing when all the conflict was going on. It was as though they were not part of the family, like they were visitors, just like the hundreds of other people that walked in and out of our home during that time. Looking back now, it makes sense because girls in our community were socialized to believe that once married, they no longer belonged in their father's home, but were fully the property of their husbands' families. As such, the wives of my father's brothers appeared to feel more at home in the family than his sisters did.

In the cold and lonely aftermath of my father's funeral, my grandmother spent a lot of time in our house. I personally did not have any problem with her. She treated me kindly, and was always doting on me and calling me *Korera*. I thought she was nice, but I did not trust her at all, mostly because I was aware that she never liked you, and I could clearly see that she did not like Lena. I saw and felt the tension, but I protected myself from it by minding my own business and staying far away from the drama.

My father's room felt cold and spooky. Because of all the stories about dead people crawling on the walls, I felt some kind of chill every time I went in there. But sometimes I found some sort of comfort there. Sometimes I went through his stuff and came across little reminders of him, and of you. He had some of your headscarves, your pictures, and your clothes. I came across his diary. It was mostly empty, but on the date of your death, he had put in an entry indicating that his "beloved" wife died on that day. I wondered if he ever called you beloved while you were still alive, struggling with your sadness and your illness.

Bonareri and I were cleaning out the room a few weeks after his burial, and we found some dirty clothes, including a few pajama pants with feces in them. We rolled them up nicely and threw them out. Neither of us said anything about it. I did not know what to feel about seeing evidence that my father was so helpless in his final days that he soiled himself. And there was no one there to clean it up for him. As we cleaned out his room, I accepted everything that I saw without thinking too much about it, without opening myself up to feeling anything about what I saw.

I took some of your headscarves. I was never going to wear them, but I wanted them anyway, maybe to feel connected to you, or maybe because there was so little physical evidence of you left in our lives. I was afraid of losing you completely.

Someone to Love

Because my father died during school break, I did not expect that anyone at school knew about it. But the moment I reported back to school in January, I realized that, in fact, almost everyone knew. The girls looked at me funny and whispered behind my back, but nobody said anything to me directly, except Anita.

Anita was a tiny, pretty, and quietly confident girl that I liked. Sometimes she subconsciously sucked on her thumb, and although it was quite a strange habit for someone our age, I thought it was cute. She was the last born in her family, and she had big sisters that wrote her letters where they referred to her as sweetie, honey, and other pet names like that. I envied her for that. My sisters never wrote me any letters, and it would be a great wonder if either of them ever used a word like sweetie to refer to me.

Anita walked over to me on the first day of school and said that she'd seen my father's obituary in the papers.
"Was that really him? Did your father die?" she asked.
"Yes," I said sheepishly, avoiding eye contact. Because I liked Anita so much, I felt all kinds of awkward around her. I could not look her in the eye. I desperately loved her, but for some reason, every time I saw her, I wanted to run away.

She said she was sorry for my loss. I said okay, and she left me alone.

Anita must have found me really confusing. It was obvious that we both wanted to be friends. I smiled at her a lot, and she responded to me warmly. I was however quickly discovering that I knew very little about real friendship that was not just about existing in the same space. The only real friend I had ever had was Peace, and with Peace it was easy because I didn't have to say or do anything. Peace was like a sister to me. All I had to do for her to like me was simply exist. With Anita, I felt like I had to be perfect, and the fear of my own imperfection made it impossible for me to be anywhere near her. I did not know how to talk to someone I liked, how to share my feelings, or share anything about myself. I was very inwardly oriented, everything made sense in my head, but I could not express myself coherently to another person, especially if it was someone I liked. This discovery greatly impacted my self-esteem. I felt unworthy of Anita's friendship.

And yet I could not help myself. I found myself thinking about Anita all the time. She was one grade level behind me, but our classes did evening prep in the same room. Every time we made eye contact, we smiled at each other. I lived for those moments.

One day, I wrote her a note, a sweet little note asking if she wanted to be best friends with me, but I couldn't bring myself to give it to her. So I put it under my mattress in the dorm. The next day, I wrote her yet another note, and another, and another. Soon

I was writing her letters, pages and pages of them. All the letters ended up under my mattress. I read them at night, wrestled with my mind about whether or not I should give them to her. I always ended up cowering under the possibility of rejection.

Anita and I continued playing our hello and goodbye game. We said hi and smiled at each other a lot. We made sure to say goodnight to each other every day at bedtime. But we never sat together to have any real conversation. The thought of sitting with her, talking to her up close, was too scary. I shuddered every time she came close to me. And that was always my cue to take off as fast as I could.

One quiet Saturday afternoon, as I was laying my laundry out on the grass to dry, I saw her walking towards me. I panicked and ran away. It was like a reflex. One minute I was airing out my laundry, and the next I was running like crazy away from this girl whom I loved so much and who seemed to have some kind of magical hold on me.

Later that day, a friend of hers told me someone found my notes and gave them to her. I wanted to shrink into myself and cease to exist. If the school hadn't been a boarding school in the middle of nowhere, I would have run away. The thought of facing her paralyzed me. How could I, knowing that she knew what was in my notes? The notes had progressed from a simple hey, let's be best friends, to a deep sharing of my most private thoughts and feelings. I wrote the notes thinking that she would never read them, but pretending that she read every one of them.

In my mind, she was already my best friend. She already knew every detail of my existence. She knew my fears, my sadness. She knew about the time my father beat you unconscious in front of me, and asked us to say our goodbyes. She knew about your prolonged illness, your constant state of weakness, your bitter emotional and physical abuse of your children, your death. She knew that I did not shed a tear when you died, that at the time, all I could think about was how glad I was that the abuse was over. She also knew that I was broken by the loss. That I missed what you could have been, but never was. I missed the hugs you could have given me, but never did, the love you could have ensured I never doubted.

In my mind, Anita also knew about my father's illness, his desperate attempts to get better by bringing into our home witch doctors and all kinds of traditional healers. She knew about the sacrificial animals that were supposed to make my father better, that ended up buried all around our home.

Because I had written her so many letters about my life, even though I never gave them to her, I imagined that Anita already knew everything about me. She knew that I was conflicted about what to feel about anything, and that because my feelings were all over the place, I felt lost, and broken.

I was in full panic mode about the letters. Now that Anita had them, I was both relieved and deeply embarrassed. Part of me was glad that she had read them, because now she could truly know me. But I was also ashamed about my life, and afraid that she would reject me, that she would think I was too broken and not good enough to be her friend.

Anita tried very hard to talk to me. Her friend assured me that she just wanted to talk to me, that she wanted to be my friend. I was too embarrassed. I kept running every time I saw her.

One evening, during night prep, Anita wrote me a note. She walked over to my desk, put it on top of the book I was reading, and walked away. Such a brilliant idea. There was nowhere to run since we were in class, and she saved me from a panic attack by writing a note rather than trying to talk to me.

The note simply said, "Yes, I want to be your best friend." I looked over at her, smiled, and mouthed "thank you". I wrote the words "I love you" underneath her words and passed the note back to her. She wrote "I love you too" and passed it back.

Weeks went by, and although Anita and I were best friends now, and we passed lots of notes back and forth, I still could not bring myself to talk to her face-to-face in the same way that I could talk to her in writing. In person, we said hi and spoke about the food, our classes, and the teachers. Anything but our lives, or our hearts. Anita did not have a past as dark as mine. She had parents who loved her, and her life was pretty much drama free. She found my stories fascinating, but she did not know what to do with them. She read the letters I continued to write to her, and drew hearts all over them. She wrote comments about how strong I was, and how everything was going to be okay. But whenever we got together in person, I was awkward and jittery. I could not wait to bolt. Anita tried to help me relax around her. She asked her other friends to tell me that she liked me a lot. That made me even more uncomfortable. I loved her but didn't know how to express love in a normal friendship.

The letters were a less awkward release. They got me through some tough days. Writing to Anita made me feel like I had a soul sister, a friend that understood my heart. I wished I could talk to her in person, hug her, cry in her arms, or just sit together in silent understanding. But I could not. She was too good for me, too graceful, too queenly, too together. Why would she want to wallow in my pain? Why would she sit with me when she had a hundred other friends? The fear of rejection was overwhelming.

Everything I did in my friendship with Anita was self-sabotaging. I was experiencing all kinds of emotions about my life during that time, and because I didn't know what to do with any of it, I overwhelmed her with all my pain, confusion, and hurt. I was practically weeping to her every single day through my letters. I also told her that I loved her all the time. She said I love you back almost every time, but I kept saying it, and telling her I want us to be even closer, and love each other even more. I had no idea why I did any of that. I just couldn't help it. I felt an intense need to love and be loved, to have someone really know and understand my heart.

One evening, I wrote Anita another one of my emotional letters. As usual I passed it to her and smiled as she was reading it. She didn't respond immediately as she usually did. This time, she did not even look at me. After a while, she took out a piece of paper, wrote on it for a few minutes, and passed it over to me.

I smiled as I opened it, expecting the usual expressions of love. What I found instead, was a stern letter, letting me know that we could no longer be friends. Anita said she felt that nothing was ever enough for me, That I was constantly seeking and seeking, and it was exhausting. She said she didn't know how else she could love me to make me feel like it was enough. So she was done.

I cannot say that I was surprised by her letter. I fully expected that people would not like me. Rejection was a more familiar feeling than the feeling of being accepted and loved. Throughout my friendship with Anita, I was waiting for the day it would all come to a crashing end. I don't know why I expected bad things to happen to me, but I was less surprised by them than by anything good coming my way.

Anita and I did not speak to each other for a while after that. I was deeply heartbroken, but I did not say anything to her about it. Instead I sat with my heartbreak, allowed it to hurt, and found solace in my writing. I also spent a lot of time reading fiction. I would lose myself in the characters' stories, and forget everything else.

Mama, while losing Anita was painful, I gained a deeper understanding of myself from that relationship. I did not realize it at the time, but Anita was the first of many problematic relationships that I had in my life. I repeated the same pattern over and over again, both in friendships and in romantic relationships later in life. I was trying to make people fill a void in my heart that was impossible to fill. It was like a curse. I loved too much, expected too much, and generally suffocated the people I loved with my need for deep connection.

Third Time Around

My relationship with my siblings was marked mainly by indifference. We each retreated into our own lives and interacted with each other at a very technical, and surface level. The fighting with my brothers subsided as we grew older, but one day, shortly after we had buried our father, my older brother, Nicco, and I had one horrible physical fight. I don't remember what we were fighting about. But I remember that my grandmother, and my aunts (your two sisters) were around. Nicco and I fought so bitterly that it took all those adults quite a good amount of effort to get us to stop. Your sisters were shocked. While it was fairly normal for siblings to fight in those days, Nicco and I both seemed to harbor so much bitterness, and our fight that day was definitely not normal. Clearly, whatever had triggered the fight was not the real reason we were fighting. I brought my personal pain into the fight, and he brought his own, and the result was a horrific show that made one of your sisters swear to never set foot in our house again. True to her word, we never saw her again until we were all fully grown adults.

Although Nicco was two years older than me, I could hold my own in a fight. I was slightly taller than him at that prepubescent age. Maybe because my emotions were so erratic at the time, I fought without any regard for anything anyone was trying to tell me. Anyone that tried to separate us got shoved aside. I did not cry at all, even though my brother hurt me just as badly as I hurt him. He, on the other hand, cried so bitterly that he ended up locking himself in a room for hours. I thought he was going to kill himself, and although that worried me a little bit, I was too angry to care.

The indifference, and sometimes hostility, continued through most of our childhood. My family was the last place I could seek emotional support. Emotions were shameful. I could never tell anyone in my family what I was feeling. And during this time, I was slowly starting to fall apart.

I did not notice Lena's illness until one day she got so ill that she could not walk. She was crawling on the floor holding her tummy due to excruciating abdominal pain. I did not know what was going on with her. I did not ask. But that familiar ache in my chest crept up and started eating at me, reminding me that I'd seen this before, that I'd walked that road twice before. And here we were again.

In my mind, I thought we were all destined to die, one by one. It seemed as though this cycle would never end. The illness, the suffering, the death.

I did not feel like I could handle it again. So I fell back on indifference. I lived my life from one day to the next, not allowing myself to feel anything. I saw things happening and accepted them for what they were, without giving any thought to them, and without thinking anything about them. I was simply existing in the world, without any desire to internalize or judge anything that was happening in it.

Lena was naturally a very skinny person. With her illness, she looked even skinnier, and people were constantly asking her what the problem was. Fortunately, it turned out that her issue was not a pernament one like my father's. Eventually she got better. This was such an unfamiliar, yet deeply reassuring outcome. I'd watched both of my parents deteriorate all the way to their deaths, so seeing someone in our family actually getting better provided hope that maybe we were not all destined to die.

The stress and tension in our house did not subside though. My brothers turned to alcohol and aggressive behavior. The younger ones also picked it up and became a constant nightmare for Lena to deal with. In addition to my brothers giving her hell, my uncles would occasionally make a point of intentionally stirring things up. One time, one of my father's brothers traveled all the way from Kisii to come to our house in Kisumu and tell us how irresponsible my sister, Lena, was. He said she was selling all of my father's properties for her own benefit, and that she was going to sell everything and leave us homeless. We listened dutifully and said nothing. I respected my uncle very much, but I did not trust him at all. Nothing he told us was news to any of us. We already knew what the family was saying, but because our father had prepared us well for this drama, we were not shaken. As much as I was not close with my sister, I trusted her fully. There was nothing my uncle could say that would make me doubt her intentions.

When he was done with us, he traveled to the university where my sister studied to repeat the same accusations to their Dean of Students. When the Dean confronted Lena about this, she lost it and took some of her frustrations out on him. I imagine the stress of the wrangles with my father's family had been building up for a while, and being accused by someone that had no idea what was really happening at home triggered an outburst.

Lena had indeed sold my father's car in order to pay her university fees. Prior to his death, our father had enrolled her at a fairly expensive private university, and with him gone, she was struggling to meet the financial obligations for that. Most of my father's vehicles had been repossessed due to non-payment. I had no idea what was happening with my father's assets. I didn't really care, but I heard stories about things being sold, and my uncle blocking our access to the life insurance that my father had taken out for us. This uncle purposely and maliciously went to the insurance company to provide information that led to the payout being rejected. As if that was not enough, he openly bragged about it and told us we would never succeed.

I stayed out of it as much as possible. I already knew that I owned nothing in that family. Everyone was selling something.

My brothers sold little things here and there to fund their new lifestyles involving alcohol and women. Lena was busy trying to ensure we remained in school and that there was food on the table. Bonareri was in the background, and honestly I had no idea what she was doing. I, well, I was existing. I was getting through the days. I didn't sell anything. I didn't do anything bad. I just quietly existed in my own little corner of the world and tried not to cause any trouble.

Doing School

After Anita, I never really got too close to anyone else at school, but I made some fairly decent friendships, and I was well liked. Anita and I spoke from time to time after healing from our little friendship break up. It was actually easier to talk to her when we were no longer friends. There was no pressure to try and impress. I told her how terribly hurt I was by her letter. She said it was necessary, that she had to put a stop to the dynamic we were building with each other. Anita was not the type to apologize when she felt justified, nor was she one to go back on her word. That door was closed, and she was very clear that she was not going to open it again.

I respected that she was able to say all that to my face while remaining so kind and friendly. Her composure, the graceful way that she carried herself, her ability to hurt me while still having such a strong hold on me, it was impossible to hold a grudge against her.

I spent a lot of my time alone, reading books mostly. Sometimes

I did want some company, but my self-esteem was so low I could not just walk up to people to hang out with them. There were girls I was comfortable around, girls that did not make me feel awkward or make me want to run when I saw them. But for the most part I did not find those girls interesting. I did not enjoy their company. And so I ended up alone most evenings and weekends while other girls were playing and chatting with their friends.

The school was divided into two sections – the classrooms section, and the boarding section – with a church in between. The classroom section was easy. We attended classes, interacted with teachers, and sometimes even bought contraband in the form of snacks from the day scholar students. I did fine in my classes, was well liked by both the teachers and my classmates, and got through the school days quite easily since there was hardly any idle time.

The boarding section was a different story. Meal times for example, could be a nightmare. Since we did not have specific visiting days, parents could visit any day, and they were allowed to bring certain foods for their children. This food (mostly fruits and juice) was then kept in the convent until meal time, when the owner was required to distribute it to others. There was no rule about whom you had to share your home food with, so most people shared with their close friends only, and ate as much of it themselves as possible. Woe unto you if you did not have friends. On days when many people were visited, it was very distressing when everyone around you got home food and snacks, and the space around your plate remained empty. The visited children went around the dining hall placing treats next to their friends' plates, and at the end of it, some students could have as many as twenty treats while others had none at all.

It was one of the most humiliating things. Some girls were kind enough to share what they got. Anita had a lot of friends, and most times, even after our friendship ended, she would share whatever she got with me. She was heaven sent, because without her, I would have spent many humiliating meal times surrounded by girls with treats while I had none.

After my father died, Bonareri visited me at school maybe once or twice. Then we had a bad fight at home and she swore never to visit me again. I couldn't blame her. She was about seven years older than me, but because I had grown taller and bigger than her by the time I was twelve, I decided that I could engage her in a physical fight. I don't remember what we were arguing about, but when she threatened to beat me up, I let her find out very quickly that I was no longer a small child. She realized that I could actually hurt her if she tried to fight me, and so she backed off. But she never set foot at my school again after that.

While I was a warrior at home, ready to defend myself at any provocation from my siblings, at school I was a totally different person. School was where the warrior in me calmed down and took a back seat, making way for the emotional, more fragile side of me to come forth. It was as though home was a war zone, and school was a retreat from all the chaos, where my soul could rest and start to heal.

One of my favorite places in the school was the church. Every time I felt lost, disappointed, sad, or lonely, I went in there and just sat on the benches. I looked at the statue of Jesus on the cross, hanging at the front center of the large building. There was a smaller statue of The Virgin Mary at the altar, and pictures on the wall representing the various stations of the way of the cross. I knew each station by heart. I could recite the rosary, and chant the multitude of prayers that we said every morning and evening. We were also required to write all the hymns by hand in a notebook.

As I sat in the church, sometimes I silently chanted various prayers. I didn't have to think about the words I was saying. Many of the Catholic prayers were ingrained in my mind and I could recite them in my sleep. I chanted the prayers because it was comforting. I needed to feel something, and the prayers helped with that a little bit. Sometimes I just sat quietly in the church and allowed my mind to be blank, to not think about anything at all. There was comfort in that too. I felt as though I was in the presence of God, a special friend that did not require words to understand what I was feeling. I didn't have to pretend with Him. I could just sit there and feel all my feelings without judgment.

And so I completed my primary school education.

Uncle Philip was there to travel with me to rural Nyanza for my first day of high school. He helped me carry my metal box as we got into an old *matatu* and set off for my new adventure at the high school. Lena paid the school fees, but didn't give me any transport or pocket money at all. So Uncle Philip personally paid for the transport, and gave me two hundred shillings for my pocket money.

The matatu was crowded and had a strong stench of body sweat mixed with other odors. Along the way, a young girl, about five or six years old, threw up on me. There was no room to get up so at least some of the vomit could roll off my clothes. The girl's mother wiped me off with a piece of cloth, but some of the vomit had seeped in and drenched me in the contents of that little girl's gut. By the time we got to school, I was a disgusting mess. But Uncle Philip proudly presented me to the school, walked with me through the registration process, and ensured I was okay before leaving to make the journey back to Kisumu.

I settled right in. At that point, I was already comfortable with boarding school life. I was independent and could take care of myself without requiring much support from anyone. I was assigned a school mother, but instead of supporting me, the girl stole my pocket money within the first day. I disconnected from her immediately since I didn't feel like I needed a school mother anyway.

The rhythm of school was easy. The girls were nice. There was really nothing to complain about, except maybe for the fact that we had to wake up at 5:30am and bathe with water that was freezing cold. Whenever I couldn't do it, I simply washed my face and went to class. My roommates didn't know that, because all three of them were serious human beings that woke up before the bell rang, bathed with freezing cold water, and were often out of the dorm before I could even convince myself to open my eyes. I accepted right from the start that I was not like them. I was never going to be one of those people that woke up before it was absolutely necessary to do so. Waking up early in the morning was a struggle for me. Bathing with freezing cold water at that hour was an even bigger struggle. At least at the primary school we didn't have to bathe in the morning. We were allowed to fetch water in our basins and leave it out in the sun all day so we could bathe with fairly warm water after our classes ended in the late afternoon.

Unlike primary school, high school was very competitive. I started off strong. I was smart, and I understood my lessons well. But I couldn't keep up with all the studying that people did outside of class. I couldn't keep up with all the homework we had to do every single day. I needed time to catch my breath, to be able to just sit and take in my new environment. But there was no time for that.

Very quickly I fell behind in my assignments. I got in trouble with my Math teacher almost on a daily basis. He would line us up - those of us that failed to hand in our homework - and give us some serious strokes of the cane. He was a bald-headed middle-aged man that seemed to take everything personally. He beat me every day with so much anger, as though I was intentionally falling behind to spite him. I couldn't take it anymore. I started skipping Math class and hiding in all kinds of odd spaces to avoid him. This meant that I fell behind even more, and by the end of the first year of high school, I was getting Es in Math. The teacher stopped bothering to ask about me. I no longer even had to hide. I would walk right out of class as he walked in, and he wouldn't say a word to me. I did not care.

Too Broken

There were good times at the High School. During the first few months in Form One, I was in a happy place most of the time, and when I wasn't, I could hide my sadness very well by withdrawing from the crowds and finding spaces where I could be alone. My classmates once unanimously called out my name as the student that best fit the description of someone who was happy and excited about life all the time. They were not wrong then. In those early months of high school, I was full of life. I made a lot of noise in class and got overly excited about the smallest things. Sometimes I would walk into class and just break into dance for no reason at all. And I wasn't even pretending to be happy. I really was excited about things, even though I could not name exactly what it was that I was excited about.

This was however immediately followed by a sudden, steep fall into sadness, and extreme fatigue. I could barely drag myself out of bed in the morning. Sometimes I pretended to be sick, just so I could sleep for a few minutes longer in the morning. I would then wake up just before the dorms were locked because I did not want to have to go to the nurse. I skipped breakfast because by the time I woke up, it was usually too late to go to the dining hall. During tea break on weekdays, we were served black tea without anything to go with it, and so if you didn't have money for bread, there was no point showing up for the ridiculously hot water mixed with tea leaves and barely any sugar. I rarely had any money, so most days I stayed hungry until lunch time.

The church at this school was outside the compound, and we were only allowed to go there on Sundays. I missed being able to sit quietly in an empty church. I had so much that I wanted to say to God. I wanted to yell at Him, scream, and cry, and demand answers. I wanted to know why me, why all the girls around me seemed to have good lives, while my whole life was a giant mess of pain and hopelessness.

On visiting days, my classmates' parents streamed in one by one, and the girls went out to meet them, spend time with them, and eat all the delicious food from home. The girls took their parents on a tour of the school, brought them to the classrooms, the dorms, and just about everywhere. There was nowhere to hide. I had to watch it all, and keep a smile on my face.

I had many friends, in the general sense of the word, but not a single close friend. I talked to many people, but didn't spend enough time with any one person to form any kind of close relationship. I think I was afraid that if people found out how broken I was, they wouldn't like me. So I gave them just enough of myself to portray the kind of positive image that I wanted them to have of me. Whenever I felt my negative side (which was mostly my sadness) coming, I would hide and deal with it alone, so that by the time I was rejoining the other students, I was a better version of myself.

One time I got fairly close to one of my classmates. She was real, and vulnerable, and did not shy away from telling me about the less than perfect aspects of her life. I was cautious, mainly because she was a Nairobi girl and it didn't make much sense to me why she would want to be my friend. Nairobi girls tended to stick together, and act superior to everyone else. This girl knew that I kept a diary, and that I wrote things in there. Maybe out of curiosity, because I did not tell her much about my life, she stole my diary and was seen reading it by another classmate. The classmate reported this to me, but when I confronted my friend, she completely denied it. I told her she was seen reading my diary, gave her every chance to come clean, but she just wouldn't own up. Eventually I told her I was done with the friendship.

Thinking back, I probably never really wanted to have a close friend then. I was too afraid of being called out for the broken mess that I felt I was. This girl gave me the perfect excuse to get out of a situation I already found quite uncomfortable. When I told her I was done, she came clean, admitted that yes, she read my diary, but was afraid to admit it because she knew I was very private about my life. She apologized, desperately, but I closed myself off and acted like what she had done to me was unforgivable. She had given me an out, so I gladly took it.

I made one other friend in that first year. This girl was very confident, even though she was an ordinary girl with nothing particularly outstanding about her looks or her grades. I was immediately drawn to her the moment I met her, mostly because she seemed very comfortable in her own skin, was solid, well put together, and bold. She was the complete opposite of what I thought I was, and she represented the kind of image that I wanted to cultivate for myself.

We got along great, but the girl was not a feelings kind of person. We both considered our friendship close, but she was not the kind of person that spent all her free time with any specific person. She showed care, but in a detached kind of way that was difficult to understand. Maybe it was her emotional unavailability that made me want so badly to be close to her. It was like Anita all over again. I started writing her letters about my life. Unlike Anita, she did not draw hearts on them or write me back. Instead, she would come right over and talk to me about whatever I'd written. Her matter of fact approach was difficult for me. But I also liked that she felt comfortable enough to discuss my life with me in person, even though she knew that I was not exactly very comfortable with those kinds of intense in person conversations.

Whenever I felt down, I would write her a letter about how I was feeling. On one such occasion, the deputy principal walked into our classroom and caught me writing a letter when I should have been studying. I was too engrossed in the letter to notice her coming in. She grabbed the letter from me, read it, and then made me read it out loud in front of the whole class. She had me lie down on the classroom floor and gave me several strokes of the cane. The pain was excruciating, but I did not dare to cry. More than it being painful, it was the most humiliating experience of my life so far.

After the deputy principal left the classroom, my friend came over to me and started scolding me for writing letters in class. She said I knew the rules, and that I should have known better. It wasn't until I received that tongue lashing from my friend that I broke down and cried. I hadn't actually cried in a very long time, but that experience, coupled with my friend's scolding, had my tears flooding down my face in front of the whole class.

"See, if you did the right thing, you wouldn't be crying right now," she said.

That was the end of my close friendship with this girl. We continued to be friendly with each other, but I never wrote her another letter, and for a long time, I never told her anything about my personal life. Amazingly, she didn't even seem to notice that I had pulled away from her. She behaved towards me the same way she had always done, claiming me as a close friend but being totally unavailable emotionally. I started to notice her less than perfect traits; she was self-righteous, highly critical of others, and intolerant of anything that she perceived as weakness or imperfection. I still talked to her, but I kept some distance to avoid her hurtful personality.

After that friendship ended, I had no one to talk to. Rather than write letters, I turned to writing stories. The stories were almost always about my life, but when I shared them, I insisted that they were fiction. People told me I was a good writer, and the recognition motivated me to write even more. Because the stories were supposedly fiction, I shared them widely. Some people openly told me they believed the stories were about me, even when I insisted they were fiction. That was annoying, but it didn't stop me from continuing to write.

My deskmate loved my stories. She was always asking for more. And I was more than happy to share. Writing was the only thing that kept me sane at that point in my life. When I wrote, I felt like my life meant something, like there was at least one thing I was really good at.

After reading a story I wrote about a young girl going through circumcision, this deskmate started calling me *ondusi*. Having spent several years in boarding schools around Luo Nyanza, I knew exactly what *ondusi* meant. She was using that word to mean that I had been cut, that a part of me was pinched off. Although the word itself could be used in many different contexts to mean different things, this girl used it to mean that I had been circumcised.

The Luo community did not practice circumcision, and since the majority of girls in that school were Luo, they used some derogatory terms (mostly more in jest than any real malice) to make fun of people from other tribes, especially Kisiis. I'd lived among Luos and gone to predominantly Luo schools all my life, but this was the first time that a Luo was directly taking a jab at me for something connected to my tribe.

Nobody had ever made fun of me in the school before, not even jokingly. My deskmate clearly thought it was a joke, but my circumcision was a sore subject for me, and it was the last thing I wanted anyone to know about me. I told her again that I wasn't circumcised, and that the story was fiction. She laughed and continued calling me *ondusi*.

I lost it. I screamed at the girl, grabbed her things and threw them across the room, then dared her to come fight me. I stood up on top of my desk and yelled at her to come at me, telling her I was not who she thought I was, and I could mess her up badly. I invited her to try me if she wanted to find out who I was. My classmates were shocked. The girl recoiled and stayed away from me from then on.

I got a reputation as the quiet but deadly girl. People stayed out of my way. I sank even deeper into my dark hole. Because of the incident with my deskmate, I stopped writing stories about my life. I actually hardly wrote anything anymore, except for school assignments. Instead, I skipped classes whenever I could. All I wanted was to sit in quiet spaces and think. There wasn't anything specific that I thought about. I just sat alone for long periods of time and allowed my mind to wander. Sometimes I fantasized about killing myself. I wondered what would happen if I did. Nobody would care. Nobody would miss me. And I wouldn't have to feel all the heartache that I felt all the time.

That familiar ache in my chest was now permanently present. It was a physical pain that wouldn't go away. I knew I wasn't sick. I knew the chest pains were a result of the internal chaos in my life. But I couldn't seem to get rid of it. I felt broken. I thought that I would never get better, that I was too broken to ever be normal again. Sometimes I wanted to die, so I could start life over again. Get another chance to have a different life. Maybe in the next life, I wouldn't have to go through the things I'd been through, the things that got me to where I was and who I was.

NO TEARS FOR THE CHERISHED

CHAPTER FIVE

Dear Mama,

I longed for you. I wasn't grieving for you in any traditional sense of the word. I didn't cry for you. I didn't spend any amount of time wishing you would come back. But there was a deep heaviness in my heart, and I knew it was because of both what I had experienced with you, and what I had not experienced with you. I kept reliving your life in my mind. I felt your every experience in my bones.

One good thing that having you constantly in my heart and mind did for me was that it humbled me a great deal. I developed more empathy, and maybe something of a "good girl syndrome". I felt a deep sense of obligation to you, to God, and to myself, to always do the right thing. While my brothers were running wild and causing chaos, I stayed on the straight and narrow, and never felt any desire to join in their shenanigans. I was terrified at the thought of being anything short of the perfect child, even though there was no one watching anymore.

Lonely

My life, both at home and at school, was very lonely. I longed for connection, and while there were a lot of people around me, I felt detached from everyone. I felt as though I lived in a parallel universe. It seemed to me as though everyone was living their lives so simply, without much baggage, but much as I tried, I could not live my life in that way. There was heaviness in my chest, and I constantly worried about everything. I didn't feel good enough to exist in any space. So I tried to make myself as small as possible.

And then there were those times when I was overcome with unexplainable excitement. The times when I was alone at home, and suddenly I would feel this gush of life in my veins, and I would jump up on top of the dining table and sing at the top of my lungs while dancing to my own off key tunes. It did not feel odd at all to me. I genuinely felt good in those moments. I was proud of myself, and my life, and who I was. My life mattered.

One time a neighbor was passing by and saw me doing this mad woman dance while singing and laughing all to myself. She watched me through the window for a while before I noticed her. I quickly jumped off the table and stood there awkwardly looking at her. She laughed and laughed, slapping her thighs every now and then at the wonders she had just witnessed.

"I didn't know you were such a *lelo*," she said when she finally stopped laughing.

In some ways I was a *lelo*. I could be extra, very extra, when I needed or wanted to be. When that happened, it was mostly in self preservation. My extraness in anger was usually when I was afraid of losing control and subsequently becoming a victim. I could not afford victimhood. My extraness in mirth was also usually an attempt to avoid losing control and becoming a victim of sadness. Whenever I felt myself becoming too lonely, or too sad, I did something outrageous, but harmless, to zap myself back to at least a neutral space. It was as though my body could sense impending danger, and in response, it could trigger my senses to respond in self-preserving ways, even if that meant acting crazy to remind myself that I was alive and okay. Losing myself completely was not an option.

While I did not feel worthy of having friends, I sought out friendships, sometimes even desperately. When I was around twelve years old, a family moved to a newly built house about two hundred meters away from where we lived, and they had a girl about my age named Maryann. Our houses were separated by a dam, a field with overgrown weeds where children played, and thick live fences. I saw her playing with her brothers outside their fence every now and then, and every time I would stand a safe distance away and just watch them, fantasizing in my head about becoming best friends with her.

Maryann's family seemed fancy. Their house was smaller than ours, but something about them reeked of class. Unlike the other children in the area, they didn't just roam around and play with whoever was outside that day. They stayed in their compound and only came out when accompanied by their parents or their aunt. Watching them through the live fence around their house was like watching one of those happy families in movies.

Showering was never a priority for me while at home. I could go a whole week without showering and feel absolutely nothing about it. Nobody in my family showered regularly, so it was never a problem. We didn't notice anybody's body odor, or any stinky breaths, probably because that was our collective reality. But when Maryann moved to the neighborhood, that reality completely changed for me. Suddenly I was showering every day, brushing my teeth, and even attempting to dress nicely. I would then go to the field next to her house and stare desperately through the fence at her playing with her family. They ignored me one hundred percent of the time and went about their games as though they didn't even see me.

One time, after waiting at the field for a while and not seeing any signs of them, I went even closer to their fence and stood there aimlessly, trying to pretend I was just an innocent passerby that had decided to hang around the area. I kept walking up and down along the fence, trying to get a peep through without appearing to do so. After doing that for over half an hour, a woman, whom I later learnt was Maryann's aunt, yelled at me through a window, asking if I was lost.
"No," I said, my heart thumping with panic and shame.
"Are you looking for something?"
"No."
"Would you like to come in?"

I could not get the words out of my mouth, but inside, I was desperately yelling "Yes please! Yes please!" I was both ashamed and relieved at the same time; ashamed that my desperation was so obvious, and relieved that I had finally been noticed by this family, and even invited to come into their home.

Maryann and I became fast friends. She didn't speak much, but like me, she was comfortable with silence. We spent a lot of time in each other's presence without needing to talk much. In some ways, Maryann was very much like my old friend, Peace. She saw my life for what it was and accepted it without question. Her home was clean and well taken care of, but she would come into our dirty, run down house and behave in it in the same way that she behaved in her own house. She sat on our dirty furniture, ate food from our dirty kitchen, and never displayed any kind of judgment.

Despite Maryann's total acceptance of the state of our family, I still felt highly insecure about the differences in our lives. I was an orphan with zero structure in my life, just existing one day to the next, and she was from a family that was probably the most structured and happy I had ever seen in my life so far.

Maryann came from a family where everybody woke up, showered, brushed their teeth, made their beds, and behaved like a family fit for TV commercials. I came from a family with no rules. Everybody existed in the same space without getting into anybody else's business. Beds were never made, the house was never cleaned, dishes were only washed when they were needed for the next meal. My siblings and I had an unspoken live and let live kind of situation. Nobody bothered anybody else.

Mama, spending time at Maryann's house made me feel very lonely. They were the kind of family that served four o'clock tea. And they served it at the table, with biscuits, groundnuts, and fruit. And they had a nice mother, a nice aunt, and brothers that behaved nicely. Her mother always insisted that I sit at the table and have tea with them. She served me the exact same thing that she served her children, and even asked if I wanted second helpings.

Maryann's family became our family friends. Her mum came to our house once to pray for us. It was the most embarrassing thing because our house was so cold, dirty, and dull, compared to theirs. But this woman did not seem to mind any of that. She came over and she prayed earnestly for our family. I saw tears in her eyes. Clearly she felt sad for us, but not at all in a condescending way. Her sadness for us felt warm and motherly, which was both comforting and depressing for me. It made the things I was missing in my life even more real and visible.

Lonely as I felt every time I was around Maryann's perfect family, I drew some hope from observing their lives. I dared to hope that one day I would have a life like that too.

Maryann's family wrote us all Christmas cards. Can you believe that, Mama? They wrote us Christmas cards! Like they actually went to the store and bought Christmas cards, wrote in them, put them in envelopes addressed to us, and delivered them to our house. It was one of the coolest things anyone had ever done for me.

Sadly, my friendship with Maryann was doomed from the start. She was too perfect, and I was too desperate, and insecure. While I fancied myself prettier than her, and this was probably true in the traditional sense of what was generally considered beautiful, she was cleaner, more polished, and she had more of a sophisticated aura about her. Maybe because she was way more confident, while I tended to shrink myself at the slightest hint of attention from anyone.

Maryann's older brother might have been an easy target when I started getting attracted to boys. But maybe because I spent so much time with their family, I did not find him in the least bit attractive. He was good looking, but more in a brotherly kind of way. Crushing on him would have been quite weird.

There was a boy though that was giving me sleepless nights. His name was Martin, and his family lived in the area. We had never spoken more than two words at a time to each other, but in my eyes, Martin was perfect. He looked like he was made from the finest heavenly clay. He was tall, light brown in complexion, with a slender but toned, and highly masculine body. He was probably about four or five years older than me, which would have made him eighteen or nineteen. The age difference was glaring, especially since he was getting into adulthood, and I was maybe fourteen years old. But I did not care. In fact, Martin being older made him even more attractive to me. His presence sent waves of excitement in my body, and I became painfully awkward whenever he so much as said hello to me.

Not that he paid much attention to me. His eyes were on my friend, Maryann. Of course. The guy followed us around every day, trying to get Maryann to talk to him. He tried striking up conversation, complimenting her, asking her random questions. Maryann wouldn't even talk to him. She treated him like he did not exist. When he showed up anywhere in our vicinity, she put on her disgusted face and refused to acknowledge him at all. Her treatment of him made me slightly uncomfortable. I was happy that she didn't want him, but unsettled by the rude way that she communicated it. She outright told him she wasn't interested in whatever he had to offer, not even his friendship.

Of course Maryann would say no to him. Any normal fourteen year old would say no to him. He was basically an adult thirsting after a child. Although he looked young, and he hung out with Nicco and other boys around that age, he was definitely at least eighteen. While that made him more attractive to me, Maryann found him disgusting. She was a good girl, the kind of girl that got saved and cried at outdoor church crusades. She actually did that once when we happened upon a crusade as we were strolling at the nearby shopping center. Maryann wanted us to stop and listen to the preaching, so we did.

The shopping center was crowded, with women selling vegetables, fish, street food, second hand clothes, and all kinds of other merchandise. Shops lined up the streets, children played near their working parents, teenagers idled in front of buildings. There was a makeshift stage at the center of an open square, and some young men and women were singing deep, inspiring praise and worship songs. When the preacher came on and started praying, a number of people in the crowd fell to the ground in tears and prayer.

The whole scene was quite normal. I'd been to lots of crusades before, and while I found them entertaining, I remained largely unmoved by them. I had a Catholic background, so church to me was supposed to be a calmer affair than it tended to be at other churches. I didn't see myself as someone that could fall to the ground because of a preacher's shenanigans. I was there mostly for the entertainment.

You can imagine how surprised I was then when Maryann walked up to the podium and broke into uncontrollable sobs. Nobody I knew personally had ever done anything like that. She was handed the microphone and she took that opportunity to confess all her sins (very minor ones, I must say), and ask for God's forgiveness. The preacher laid hands on her head as she cried, prayed for her, and invited her to give her life to the Lord. Right there, at the open air, roadside crusade, my fancy friend, Maryann, gave her life to the Lord. I saw a more vulnerable side of her that I had never seen before.

We walked back home together when the crusade was over. Maryann acted like nothing out of the ordinary had happened.

In fact, she talked about a lot of other things, but did not at all address her newly acquired salvation. I played along and talked about whatever she was talking about. The crusade became one of those things that never happened. Maryann continued being her sophisticated self, and I continued being her less than perfect side kick.

Maryann was not the kind of girl that needed to be loved by a boy like Martin. She probably was not the kind of girl that needed to be loved by any boy at all at that stage in her life. But I was definitely in need of love. I had none at home, and Martin seemed like he could be the love of my life.

Because Martin was paying zero attention to me, I set out to pursue him. Just like I had done numerous times before with people I was desperate to connect with, I wrote him letters. Dozens of letters, which I kept hidden in my room because I did not have the courage to send them. He became my new obsession. I thought about him all day, every day, and I spoke to him in my letters as though we were already in love with each other.

One day, I felt brave, and so I wrote a special letter, professing my love for Martin and asking him to be my boyfriend. It was a letter I had written many times before, but on this day, I was not going to chicken out and hide it in my room. So I read it and reread it over and over again to make sure it was perfect, and then I gave it to a little boy from the neighborhood to pass on to Martin.

It was the longest day of my life. In my mind, I expected Martin to show up at my house, any time, and take me into his arms. I expected he would fall head over heels in love with me, and apologize for never having paid attention to me before. That did not happen. Instead I spent the next few days in heart wrenching pain, not knowing what Martin was thinking. The little boy assured me that he had personally given the letter to Martin. I even made him secretly point out the exact guy he had given the letter to so I could be sure he gave it to the right person.

He got the letter alright. Martin became ice cold to me. Whereas before he'd treated me with polite indifference, he switched to acting like I did not exist, much like Maryann treated him. He stopped saying hello to me, and would completely ignore me when we bumped into each other.

That was my first real heartbreak. I sat with the shame for a long time. It was humbling. I realized that even though I was probably prettier than Maryann, she was more desirable than I was. At least to Martin. And if I was being honest with myself, she was probably more desirable, period. I was pretty, but I was damaged, and I didn't have much in terms of personality. The rejection from Martin made me take a long honest look at myself, and I recognized the many flaws that I had. While this rejection could have very easily made me reject myself as well, it made me embrace myself that little bit tighter. Because of the amount of time I spent sitting in my shame and having an honest conversation with myself about this situation, I developed some empathy and compassion for myself. I realized that I could admit that I was deeply flawed, but still love myself fiercely.

It also helped that I had several boys in the neighborhood that would give anything to be seen with me. None of them were anywhere near being as attractive as Martin, but it still boosted my ego that they went to great lengths to try and get my attention. One of them even serenaded me with love songs outside my kitchen window. I was desperate for love, yes, but I still had some standards.

Eventually, after weeks and weeks of ignoring me and allowing me to languish in agonizing shame, Martin finally sent me a verbal message through my brother, Nicco. This was even worse than saying nothing at all. He told my brother that he was really disappointed in me because I knew very well that he was interested in my friend Maryann, and yet I went ahead and wrote him a love letter.

It was like turning the dagger that he had already stuck in my heart weeks before. Of all the people he could have told, he chose to tell my brother. And of course my brother told everyone else in our family. I pretended not to care, but my ego was deeply bruised. I discovered what a heartbreak felt like, and it was made even worse by the fact that everyone in my family knew about it. It would have been better if Martin had ignored me and my letter forever.

I found some comfort in the knowledge that at least he didn't tell Maryann about it. Maybe he would have if she gave him the time of day, which she never did. Maryann would never even let him open his mouth to tell her anything about me.

Fortunately, or unfortunately, my friendship with Maryann was already on a slow decline. We still talked from time to time, but our conversations had become awkward. I felt too guilty to spend time with her. Of course I couldn't tell her what had happened between me and Martin. It was too embarrassing. And I tried to convince myself that I shouldn't feel guilty because they weren't dating, and she didn't even like him. But I still felt like I had somehow betrayed her. Martin certainly thought that I had done something wrong. So I distanced myself from both of them and allowed my friendship with Maryann to die out slowly over time.

Crumbling

Mama, when I look back at life in the years after our father died, the word that comes to mind is crumbling. Everything came apart. Every day was worse than the previous. Most of our relatives disappeared, and the ones that stayed were there mostly because they were trying to benefit financially from our assets, or they were trying to cause some kind of trouble.

My grandmother decided that the house she used to sleep in sometimes when she visited our family was now hers to own, and she took it over fully. It was a small one bedroom guest house that was right next to the main house. My grandmother insisted that my father built that house for her, and so she put a tenant in there and collected rent from them religiously every month. Needless to say, we never saw a cent of that rent money.

Mama, I could say that I don't know why my grandmother liked me, but I think it is rather obvious. I personally never had any tensions with her, maybe because I was a child at the time, but more likely because she had more bones to pick with my sisters, both of whom were technically her step grandchildren. This fact was never discussed openly. It was a non issue in our family because neither you nor our father ever mentioned it while you were alive. But I imagine it must have been an issue in my grandmother's head all along. She openly told me that I was the only one she liked in that house. She also told my brothers to beat up my sisters if they did anything to deserve it.

The boys felt powerful. Everything about where we were in our lives indicated to them that they were superior to the girls. My father had left all his property to them, and every conversation regarding our family within the extended family included them more than it included us. We, the girls, were seen as temporary family members. And our brothers started treating us as such. A common idea that got thrown around was that the girls would eventually get married and leave. And so the only people that truly belonged there were the boys.

My oldest brother, Paul, was supposed to start his third year of high school, but he decided that he'd had enough of school, and he dropped out. Pleading with him to go back to school was like playing music to a deaf goat. Lena tried, but because she had never had a chance to establish herself as an authority in our family, nobody listened to her. Even I knew that I did not have to listen to her. She could not beat me like my mother used to. And that's how Lena lost the education battle with my brother. He fancied himself grown, and he had friends who drank the kinds of illicit alcoholic brews that could only be handled by grown men. And so he too became a grown man.

A young woman joined our family as my brother's wife. Initially, it was exciting to have a new sister-in-law, although she never paid any attention to me. She was tall, loud, and fairly huge, definitely bigger than my brother physically. She moved around the house like we didn't exist, like she was the queen, and our house her castle. It became obvious quickly enough that she was not interested in building any kind of relationship with us. The only person she could see in that house was Paul.

The young woman immediately became the evil sister-in-law that stirred the proverbial pot every chance she got. Not that my brother wasn't messed up enough all on his own before she showed up, but she certainly didn't help. She was a young woman who, like Paul, had just dropped out of school and was ready for a crazy lifestyle. Luckily for her, she landed in a family where nobody held anyone else accountable for anything, and that was perfect for the young and hot blood that ran through her veins.

My brother demanded his share of my dad's property, specifically the title deed of our estate in Busia, which apparently my father left to him. When my father died, Lena kept all the documents with the intention of handing them over to my brothers when they came of age. Paul was certainly not yet ready to handle his own title deeds. He was a high school dropout, a drunk, a lost soul, with an equally lost young woman by his side. Lena refused to hand him his title deed and instead tried to persuade him to go back to school.

Paul was not trying to hear any of that. He was a gentle soul when sober, and the only way he could stand up to Lena was by doubling down on the drinking. He would stay out all day and half the night, then show up drunk out of his mind, with a mouth full of death threats. Together with his girlfriend, they terrorized Lena and threatened to beat her up if she didn't hand over the title deeds. Lena tried to stand her ground, although she was terrified. Eventually, they gave her an ultimatum; hand over the title deed within twenty four hours or get killed. That was her cue to get out of there. She fled home and went to live with a friend.

After the twenty four hours had elapsed, Paul came home so drunk he could barely stand. He was ready for war. He stumbled into the house, his girlfriend in tow, and went from room to room yelling out Lena's name. Lena was nowhere to be found. My sister, Bonareri, and I sat there quietly. When he realized that Lena had fled, Paul threw a tantrum and called Bonareri all kinds of insulting names. He blamed her for allowing Lena to run away, and said it was now up to her to produce that title deed. He gave her twenty four hours.

The next evening, Bonareri took her dinner early and hid herself in our bedroom. The bedroom lock was broken, so she had to push the cupboard against the door, and everything else that she could find to ensure that it wouldn't be easy for my brother to get in the room. I stayed in the living room because so far, none of his anger had been directed at me. I did not know anything about his title deeds.

As usual, Paul came back home drunk out of his mind. I was the only one in the room when he walked in.

"Where is Bonareri? Where is my title deed?" he yelled.
"I don't know," I said.

He went up to our room and tried to open the door. He couldn't. He was too drunk to walk through an open door without falling over himself, let alone a door with a cupboard against it on the other side. His girlfriend's specialty was mostly lighting fires behind the scenes. She just stood there watching him struggle with the door and offered no help at all.

When Paul couldn't open the door, he made me his next target. He yelled at me and insulted me for a good half hour. He was well aware that there was no way I even knew where his title deed was, but since he was drunk and his tongue was loose under the influence, he took the opportunity to vent his frustration. He said he was going to kill everyone in that house, and that he would cut us all into small pieces if we didn't give him his title deed.

I was generally scared for my life on a daily basis at home. I did not doubt that my brother could actually kill us given the right circumstances. The fear of being killed at home was not new. It was a fear I'd had all my life. It manifested in a constant dull ache in my chest, and became more of a pounding whenever the danger was more immediate.

As my brother swore and cursed at me, it was more of the dull ache that I felt. I knew he was too drunk to kill me right there and then. And I'd also done a quick calculation of my surroundings and was confident that there was nothing around that he could use to kill me. Unless he snuck up on me from behind or otherwise caught me unawares in some way. But as long as I kept him within view and at a fair distance from where I was, the immediate danger was minimal at best.

The next morning, I felt more afraid than I did the previous night. I knew how badly Paul wanted his title deed, and it was clear that given an opportunity, he could very well chop us up into pieces. So I woke up early and went to town to find my uncle Philip at the gas station where he worked. He was still the only adult that seemed even mildly concerned about us.

I told Uncle Philip everything. I don't know what exactly I expected him to do, but somehow I expected that he would have a solution to my problem. He listened carefully to the stories about what was happening at home, occasionally getting up to go serve a customer. When I was done, he asked a colleague to cover for him, took me to a nearby fast food restaurant, bought me a plate of fries and two sausages, then left me there to eat by myself after reassuring me that my brother cannot kill me. Watching him walk away was the loneliest feeling. I needed an adult to come home with me, and as I watched Uncle Philip leave me at the restaurant in my moment of fear, emotional exhaustion, and desperation, it finally sank in that he could never be my father, however much I longed for him to be. I felt more alone than ever before.

That evening, when Paul got back home, he said he knew I'd gone to report him to Uncle Philip. I have no idea how he knew, but it was probably obvious after the trauma of the previous night that Uncle Philip would be the person I ran to for help. He was practically the only adult in our lives at the time that was not trying to hurt us or take something from us. Paul said if I ever reported him to anyone again, he would beat me up so badly I would not be able to recognize myself.

Lena ended up giving Paul his title deed. It was clear that we would not know peace in that house until he got what he wanted. As soon as he got the title deed, he left us alone and redirected his focus to having fun with his girlfriend and his crazy friends. His friends were constantly drunk and loud, and they fancied themselves really cool. They'd go to nightclubs and concerts, and pretend they could rap like the famous rappers whose pictures my brother cut out of newspapers and stuck on the walls in his room. They would hang out in a group and act super fresh. All the young boys wanted to be like them, and the girls wanted to be with them. I watched from a safe distance. Paul's friends were way out of my age range, and they were scary.

My brother started smoking cigarettes. It seemed like such a bold thing to do, and he did it very openly, because of course nobody could dare say anything about it to him. He got arrested once or twice for various minor crimes, and every time my sister Lena got him out of jail.

Mama, I can imagine how painful it must have been for you to look down on earth and see your son spiraling out of control like that. It was distressing for me as well, but I felt helpless. I accepted it as our new reality, and I also accepted that there was nothing I could do about it.

My other brother, Nicco, also started going down the same path. He would often get in trouble at school, and Lena would have to go sort his issues out. One time, one of your younger brothers, our uncle, went to Nicco's school because of some kind of trouble that Nicco had gotten himself into. The boy's discipline was so lacking that, from stories I heard later, he ended up not only insulting our uncle but also attempting to fight him physically.

I watched the craziness my brothers were unleashing on the world without allowing too much of it to get to me. I was sad that they were doing all those things, but I was also very aware that there was nothing I could do about it. After years of internalizing their issues, I got to a place where I disconnected for my own sake. Whatever they chose to do was no longer my problem unless someone physically laid their hands on me. And for a long time nobody did. I was fine. I was invisible. I lived my life quietly and let them live theirs any way they saw fit.

One day I came from boarding school to a terrifying scene at home. It was in the middle of a school term, and we'd been sent home because there was a nationwide teachers' strike. As soon as I got to the door, I knew something was wrong. The glass on the door was broken and I could see blood in the house. I wanted to turn around and run. But where would I run to? There was nowhere else to go. Short of sleeping outside in the cold, that house was the only shelter I had. And so I walked through the broken door and stepped into the house. There was broken glass everywhere. And blood. Splatters of blood all across the floor.

The first thought that crossed my mind was that one or both of my sisters were dead. I didn't even have to think about who did it. My brother, Paul, was always threatening to kill someone in that house, and I was afraid he had finally made good on his word.

The curtains were open and I could see that some of the glass on the floor was from the broken windows, and some from broken utensils in the kitchen. In addition to the blood and the glass on the floor, everything seemed to be scattered everywhere. It was as though someone had rummaged through the house, throwing everything they could lay their hands on all over the place.

I spent about two minutes in the house before deciding that it was not safe for me to be there. It seemed and felt eerie in there.

I felt as though someone was going to show up at any moment and chop my head off. So I went outside and sat under a tree. I didn't have a plan. I just sat there aimlessly and thought nothing, felt nothing. I just existed there, under that tree, with no idea what I was going to do.

After a long while, a woman came through the gate. She lived in one of the *mabati* houses in our compound. She said hello and sat down across from me. I asked if she knew where my family was. She said she didn't. She went on to tell me that my brother got into a fight with one of his friends and somehow stabbed the friend with a knife. Thankfully, the guy didn't die. But he came back with a gang of his friends and they trashed our house. Everyone in my family escaped alive. But the neighbor said none of them had been back since.

I sat under that tree for a few more hours, then decided to go to Uncle Philip's place of work. I didn't know where else to go.

Uncle Philip came back to the house with me. We found my brother Nicco there. He too had just come from boarding school and found the same mess that I found. Uncle Philip paid one of the neighbors to clean the house up for us. He put cardboard boxes on the broken windows, got padlocks for the doors, then said he had to leave. I wanted to cling to him and cry until he said he would take me with him. But I didn't. Instead I nodded when he said everything would be fine, and that we should just lock the doors and sleep.

He left, and I did the only thing that I could do; I suppressed my fear, accepted that I had zero control over what could happen to me in that house, and went to bed.

Paul did not come back to that house for years after that incident. He moved to Busia and started a new life at our old home with his girlfriend.

Our Kisumu house degenerated very fast after that. The broken windows were never fixed, and everything else fell apart in very quick succession. The ceiling board started to rot and fell in at several points in the house, including right above the bed in our room. The electricity was disconnected for lack of payment, and so we started using tin lamps, which discolored the walls and the ceiling, making them soot dark. Since there were no adults in the house, we did not clean anything. There was no one to make us do it, and none of us was motivated to try and keep a clean house. When the place got disgusting enough I would go out of my way and clean it, but I did so grudgingly because my brothers could never be bothered to make the slightest effort.

The toilets in the house were non-functional, because we never had running water, and could only afford to buy water by the jerrycan; just enough to cook and maybe shower every now and then. We used a pit latrine outside, but even that gave way and fell in on one side. We had to continue using it anyway because it was the only toilet that we had. We would pee outside, and whenever we had to go for number two, we would either wear our hearts in our sleeves and go in there, despite the risk of falling into a pit latrine, to do our business. Alternatively, and this is a trick that my brothers came up with, we would find a private location, poop on scrap paper, carry it into the latrine, and quickly deposit it into the hole before the floor could fall in. This was a much safer option, and one that I personally preferred. Though generally humiliating, it was much less scary to poop on scrap paper than to risk falling into a pit latrine.

In addition to the house falling apart, we got some interesting animal visitors who decided to come live with us. Some animals made a home for themselves in our ceiling, and every night, and sometimes during the day, they would run, walk, or crawl across the ceiling. I was terrified. Before we knew what was up there, we thought it might be the witchcraft stuff my father used to talk about during his illness. And since we didn't talk to each other much, we each endured our terror quietly and privately. I would stay up late at night listening to the sounds and expecting some kind of ghost to charge at me any time. I would only fall asleep in the early hours of the morning, out of pure exhaustion.

Eventually we figured out that we had monitor lizards up there. Sometimes we saw some strange animals on the roof that looked like leopards. They were not really leopards, but they looked a lot like leopards. Other people saw the animals too, and different people had different things to say about that situation. Most of our neighbors were scared of the animals, and probably thought it was witchcraft. The few who actually had the guts to come talk to us about it said it was probably our dead parents coming back in animal form to look after us.

The leopard-like animals were harmless. They went on the roof every now and then, stretched themselves out to bask in the sun, and then disappeared, maybe into the ceiling.

The animal that scared me the most was the crawling one. I could deal with leopard lookalikes, and monitor lizards, but there were also some things up there that crawled. And because there was a big hole in the ceiling, right above my bed, I was terrified that a crawler would one day fall on me as I slept. We covered the hole by stuffing some old clothes in it, but the hole was too big, and obviously the clothes could not help much in preventing an animal from falling through.

I remained terrified, but continued to sleep on that bed, sometimes with my sisters, and sometimes alone if they were away. There was nothing I could do about it. The room was too small to move the bed. Sleeping in the living room was even more terrifying, with all the broken windows, the darkness, and the vast space. My father's old room was out of the question. His things were still in there, together with all the things from his office. The room looked and felt creepy, like it was home to a ghost. The only other room was my brothers' room, which was in worse condition than ours. The other side of the house was rented out.

The fence behind our house was overgrown, and nobody was paying any attention to keeping it trimmed. So the space between the fence and the house became narrower and narrower. We could no longer sit back there for fear of our animal roommates.

One day, I stuck my head out of our bedroom window and saw a giant python crawling on the back wall of our house. It was one of those snakes that could easily swallow a person, or even a cow, whole. I'd heard before that the snake had been spotted in the general area before, and so when I saw it behind our house, my body did not react in shock. I slowly and quietly pulled my head back into the house, closed the window, and never told anyone about it for a very long time.

Thinking back on it, I was too traumatized at that point in my life to have any other reaction. I had seen it all at that point. I was practically surviving moment to moment, without any idea what was going to become of me. Even if I wanted to tell someone about it, there was no one to tell. My sisters did not live at home most of the year, and my brothers were almost never home until late at night. I sat at home in solitude and just tried to get through the days.

Sometimes I woke up in panicked horror from tormenting snake-related nightmares. Still, I did not tell anyone about the python. I was afraid that speaking about what I had seen would make it even more real. In my mind, keeping quiet about it meant that maybe I was mistaken, maybe the python wasn't really there. I knew that I had nowhere else to go. I had to sleep in that house. And the only way I could sleep in that house was if I pretended that the python did not exist. And that somehow, there was a higher power protecting me from the animals living in our ceiling.

Falling in Love

Boarding school was my saving grace. When I was in school, I knew that I was safe, even when I was sad and depressed. Nobody there was trying to kill me. There were no strange animals living above my head. And so I could sleep at night without worrying that I could die at any moment.

That didn't take away from the fact though that I was an emotional mess. I didn't know how to connect with anyone. I had friends, but I was not available for friendship. I was too much in my own head, in my own hurt and sadness. And the kind of people that reached out to me were the kind of people I had no kind of interest in becoming friends with. I kept them close enough that if I needed them to do something for me, I could count on them to help, but also far enough that I didn't really have any friendship obligations to them.

I still had the tendency to fixate and obsess about specific people. The kind of people that I obsessed about did not seem to have any interest in me. They maybe said hi once in a while, but none of them actively tried to be my friend. I recognized that I had a pattern of longing for connection with people who were emotionally unavailable to me, and ignoring people who were eager to be my real friends. But I couldn't help myself. I just constantly found myself chasing one person or the other for their love and attention.

The first boy that I loved instantly when we met, and that fell in love with me just as hard, was Oscar. I'd been in the drama club for over a year, been to many school outings where we mingled with boys from many different schools. But no boy that I considered attractive had ever shown interest in me. And so when I was introduced to Oscar, I didn't expect he would be interested in me. He was tall enough that I had to look way up at him, and he was muscular - definitely my kind of attractive. We were introduced by a girl in my class that I liked a lot, but that I could never gather the courage to befriend because she was way too cool, and per my own judgment, way too good for me.

For some reason, we happened to be hanging out together during that school outing, and when Oscar came over to say hi to her, she introduced us. Our eyes locked, and I quickly looked away, all flushed with sudden feelings of excitement and dread.

About a week after this meeting, I was pleasantly surprised to receive a letter in the mail from Oscar. I rarely received any letters in the mail. The only person that ever wrote to me was an old friend from primary school that had become somewhat of a penpal. While we were never close back in the day, we developed some kind of bond in the final days before graduating from primary school, and agreed to keep in touch through letters. My penpal friend was very smart in primary school and ended up going to a national school, the kind of school where the best academic giants in the country, based on the Kenya Certificate of Primary Education examinations, went to. I didn't expect that our promise to keep in touch would hold, but writing to and reading from this girl turned out to be quite a rewarding experience. She was the first person I had ever met in my life that could match my depth in self expression. Her letters were deep, personal, and all around beautiful. They got me through some really difficult days. I didn't think anyone could get me as much as this penpal did until Oscar came around and not only met but far surpassed my expectations in just how deep he was willing to go. I was in emotional heaven. Finally I had met someone that could speak to my soul.

Oscar was a beautiful writer. I had never seen a boy write so beautifully. Reading his long, and oh so beautiful love letters, made me blush and feel all kinds of warm inside. The girl that introduced us seemed jealous for a little while, maybe because she'd wanted him for herself, but in time, she became more supportive of our relationship and even became a friend.

I lived for the letters from Oscar. For the first time in my life, I felt that someone truly, and deeply loved me. He really did. Maybe even more than I loved him. And I loved him a lot. He wrote to me every week without fail, regardless of whether I responded or not. He was in his school's drama club as well, so we met quite a number of times during school outings. It was usually in open spaces, and so all we really got to do was hang out and talk. I felt very comfortable with him. He had this special ability to give me butterflies and goosebumps, without making me want to flee from him. Maybe because of the depths of emotion we had gone to with each other, I felt that he knew the real me, and he accepted me for who I was.

We were lucky enough that about a year after we met, both of our teams made it to the nationals in the country's drama festivals. And because our schools were in the same county, we got to travel together, maybe around ten hours on the road, to Nyeri. It felt like the best ten hours of my life. We started off separated, boys on one side, and girls on the other, but as we went along, we mingled up and I got to sit next to him. We talked for hours, and I felt as though we were truly connected on a spiritual level. He understood me, and that was a lot, because not many people in my life understood me. In fact, I could probably say that nobody in my life at the time understood me at all.

We spent about a week in Nyeri. We were housed in different schools, so we only got to see each other during the day. But they were such beautiful days. We spent a lot of time together, talked and talked until we felt like we knew everything about each other. I truly felt like I was living my best life. I never wanted to stop feeling the things that I was feeling with Oscar.

On the final night in Nyeri, the events ran long because they had to announce all the winners and wrap up the competitions. Darkness fell, and we were still at the venue of the event, which was separate from the schools where we slept.

We noticed that students were scattering to many different parts of the compound, and so we moved away too and walked towards where the school buses were parked. As all this was happening, the lights went out. It wasn't uncommon to have blackouts, so no big deal. Instinctively, Oscar and I held hands. No words were said, he just took my hand into his, walked me over to a tree that was next to one of the buses, and took me in his arms. I started to melt into his big frame, and when he kissed me, I was completely done, finished. I was like a rag doll, and I felt like I was floating in space, with no control whatsoever of my body. I had never felt that in my life, never been kissed before, never had any kind of experience in my life that was anywhere close to what I felt in that moment.

I clung to him, almost desperately. I cried. I could not believe I was there, that I was having this absolutely mind blowing experience, in the arms of someone that I loved. Looking back, I had never even hugged a boy before. This right here, under a tree, surrounded by darkness, and school buses, and dozens of other young couples like us, was my initiation into the world of being in an intimate relationship with a boy.

Before I had time to fully take that moment in, a flashlight shone on our faces, and we heard a woman yelling at us. It was a teacher from a different school. Oscar and I quickly jumped away from each other and tried to pretend we were just standing there. The woman said she'd seen our faces and she was going to report us to our teacher. As it was, there were a lot of couples in the same vicinity, doing exactly the same thing we were doing, and as this teacher yelled and shone her flashlight around, trying to catch their faces, a number of people took off in many different directions. We were not to be left behind. As we ran, I saw a number of girls from my school also running away with their boyfriends.

When the event ended and we got on the bus, our teacher got on the bus and said we were not going anywhere until we told him which students were making out near the buses. He got off the bus to give us time to find the culprits and hand them over to him. Oscar was on a different bus since we were being transported to different schools for the night. I signaled for him to come over. He came to the window near where I was seated. I whispered to him not to say anything, and to deny everything no matter what, should his name come up.

"Who, me?" he said, feigning surprise. "I have no idea what you are talking about. I was in the hall the whole time."

We laughed, and he went back to his bus. I was confident he would never betray me, because doing so would mean he was getting himself in trouble as well. Besides, he cared about me too much to get me into trouble.

Most people on that bus knew it was I whose face was seen clearly by the teacher. But nobody was going to say my name. Instead someone came up with the idea that we could say it was one of the younger girls in form two. She had been seen by several people making out with a boy. Her name was thrown out there and everyone immediately agreed that she would be the one to be handed over to the teacher. She was an easy target because she was a form two, and most of us were form threes. And also she was a newer student, having transferred from a different school. Nobody cared how she felt about the whole situation. She sat there quietly and listened to a group of girls making decisions about her without so much as acknowledging her presence.

When the teacher came back to the bus, she was handed over as the culprit. As she got up to go and wait for the teacher outside, she looked at me and made a cut throat sign to let me know that she knew it was my name that should have been given up. I shrugged and mouthed the word sorry. I knew that she wouldn't dare give me away. It would be easier for her to take whatever punishment the teacher gave her, than deal with a whole group of girls that could be all kinds of cruel. The poor girl took the fall for all of us, and continued to take the fall at school when we returned and the story went around. People would make kissing sounds and burst out laughing whenever she got into a form three classroom. She braved it for as long as it lasted, and never once tried to implicate me in that story. Mama, sometimes I think about that girl, and I just want to give her a hug.

Hot and Cold

The high from being in love was intoxicating. I visited Oscar at his house during the holidays, and he came over to our house often. I was not shy about introducing him to everyone, including my siblings, as my boyfriend. He was a real catch; handsome, confident, and from a respectable national school; and I was very proud to be associated with him. Besides, I felt grown. I was sixteen years old, and at that age, I no longer thought there was any shame in having a boyfriend. We spent a lot of time together. He gave me serious butterflies every time he touched me. It was a feeling like none I had experienced before in my life, and I wanted to hold on to him as tightly as I could, for as long as I could.

I realized quickly enough that as much as I was enjoying this new experience of being loved by a boy, an old fear was reawakening. Naturally, Oscar was trying to get more than a kiss here and there from me. The harder he tried, the more I shrunk into myself and pushed him away. The trauma of my circumcision was coming back to the surface. For one thing, I was afraid he would find out that I was cut, and that he would leave me because of it. That was a thought I had never had to grapple with before, because I had never been in a situation where the possibility of someone finding that out about me was real. Besides, while I felt ready for a boyfriend in my life, I was certainly not okay with that level of intimacy. Oscar let it go as soon as he noticed my panic and discomfort. I explained that my hesitation was a result of my personal principles and my religious beliefs. He found the idea that he was dating a girl of good morals highly attractive.

What I told Oscar about having all these principles was true in some ways. It was more fear than principles, but I did have rules about what I could and could not do at that stage of my life. I had seen a lot of out of control youth in my family and neighborhood, and I was absolutely never planning on taking that path. Alcohol, drugs, partying, sex… none of that appealed to me. My biggest fear was contracting HIV, or getting pregnant and ruining my chances of having a successful life. I was also terrified of disappointing you and my father, even though you were both dead. Somehow I felt that you would know if I did something bad or shameful, and that alone was enough to keep me on the straight and narrow.

Oscar was okay with the limitations I put on our relationship. He was impressed by my ability to remain good despite the fact that I practically had no one to answer to. I could do anything I wanted with myself, and I was choosing to be good. He said he was going to make me his wife one day. I believed him. We were soulmates, happy to spend hours and hours just talking, and imagining a future together.

My relationship with Oscar brought me some unwanted attention from my sisters. Being the invisible child in the family, I was not used to people talking about me or paying me any kind of mind. But because I was spending a lot of time with Oscar, my sister, Bonareri, decided that this meant I was crossing over to the dark side. I understand now that she was looking out for me, but being the kind of person that she was at the time, she came at me with wild accusations, not only about Oscar but also about every other male person that she saw me talking to. She said my friends were HIV positive, and that I would soon die of AIDS if I kept hanging out with them. Most of those boys were boys from a church I went to at home, and I spent considerable amounts of time with them because we were all in the church's drama group. I had absolutely no interest in a relationship with any of them. Bonareri had a hard time believing that. I did not feel the need to justify myself to her, especially since she was accusing rather than asking.

Lena also seemed to be looking at me sideways whenever she saw me with a boy. Since she was hardly ever around, she didn't get to meet Oscar. One time though, she saw me sitting outside in the dark with one of the boys from the neighborhood. He was kind of a bad boy, maybe a little childish too, but I liked talking to him. When Lena saw me with him, she immediately assumed there was something going on with us, and she made a sarcastic remark about it when I came back inside.

"I see you've also started," she said.

Mama, her words reminded me of something you used to say when any of us did something that mirrored our father's behavior. You would give them a stern look and simply say, *"fuata nyayo"*. Those words were heavy, because they meant that the person was following in my father's footsteps, and that was never a good thing coming from you.

This sudden attention from my sisters was frustrating. I did not at all see Lena or Bonareri as parent figures or guardians to me. They barely knew anything about me. Before I got a boyfriend, I was invisible to everyone in that house. Nobody even knew how I was doing in school. No one ever asked for my report card, nobody knew if I had any friends in school or not, if I was okay or not. Nobody cared until they saw me in a relationship. Thinking back on it now, Mama, maybe I was invisible because I was a good child. Nobody expected that I could do anything bad, and so they did not have to think about me or pay any attention to me. Having a boyfriend, and several male friends, was perhaps the first indication my sisters got that I might have the potential to stray from my self-imposed straight and narrow path.

What they did not know was that I was in no danger at all, at least not the kind that they had in mind. In fact, I was experiencing an important shift in my life, and in the way that I perceived myself. Being with Oscar taught me that I was loveable, and worthy. He was the one bright spot in my life at a time when everything else seemed to be falling apart. He saw my life with all its imperfections, chaos, and brokenness, and still chose to love me as though I was really something. That was some kind of love that I had never experienced before, and for a good while, I basked in it.

Until I started to feel unworthy again.

The depression came back in waves. When I was in school, I missed Oscar a lot, and the letters he wrote to me no longer seemed enough to fill the emptiness that I often felt in my quiet time. I started to feel like Oscar was too good for me anyway. I told myself that there was no way he could love me the way that he said he did. And so I slowly started to pull away from him.

He continued to write me letters every week. Sometimes I wrote back, and sometimes I didn't. I went back to skipping classes, and picking fights with teachers I didn't like. Skipping class led to skipping church, which in my school, was one of the worst things anyone could do.

Church had been one of my favorite places to be; a place where I felt connected to something, or someone way bigger than me. But even that connection soon became painful. I was angry at God. The reality of my life became so painfully clear to me, and I felt that everyone around seemed to have a decent life, while my life was a mess. I felt empty. I was in pain, and I didn't understand why I had to be in so much pain, why God allowed for my life to be the way that it was.

And so when other people woke up on Sunday mornings to go to church, I stayed in my bed and slept.

The dorm prefect decided to report me for skipping church. She didn't warn me that she intended to do so, but I knew all along that there was no way I could miss church for weeks on end and not get reported. Even with knowledge of the possible consequences, I just couldn't gather the energy to get out of bed and go to church anymore.

The deputy principal was a small, harsh woman that had a permanent sneer on her face. She seemed to be suffering from some kind of superiority complex, looking down on everything and everyone. One morning she stood in front of the school during morning assembly and announced that she was disgusted by the behavior displayed by some of us. She said "some people" had decided they will no longer be Christians, and will therefore not go to church. She then went on a rant about those "some people" that did not have respect for the school or for God, and concluded that non-believers did not belong in that school.

After she was done, she called out my name and said I should go see the principal immediately after assembly.

I'd never been to the principal's office before. Although I'd done many things over the years that might have landed me there, none of those things had escalated to that level. I was terrified. And humiliated because now the whole school knew that I'd been skipping church.

The moment the principal walked into the room and asked if I was the one that had decided not to go to church, I broke down into tears. I'd been sitting in her office for about twenty minutes waiting for her, and during that time I'd done some personal reflection to try and figure out how I got there. What was happening to me, and how was it that I was landing at the principal's office for behavior issues? I did not want to be that person, but then here I was.

The principal seemed surprised by my tears. As she stood there staring at me, my sobs became deeper and heavier, like a load that had been sitting on my chest for a long time, and was finally shedding. I wasn't used to crying. My life didn't give me many opportunities to cry. And so this sudden gush of tears was a surprise to me as well. And a relief. The principal was an elderly nun with a kind but tired face, and a deep Luo accent. She sat down behind her desk, let me cry for a while, then asked what the problem was. I told her I was just feeling really sad, and that I couldn't cope with everything that was happening around me.

She had a hard time understanding what exactly my problem was.

"What do you mean you are sad? Did something happen to you?"
"No."
"Is it because you are an orphan?"
"No. I just feel tired."
"Tired of what?"
"I don't know," I cried. "I'm just really tired."

The principal was confused. She didn't know what to do with me, especially because I was supposed to be in trouble, and here I was falling apart in her office. Beating me didn't seem like an appropriate response. Instead she told me to go back to class, and ensure I see the school counselor during my free time. She also said she should not hear about me skipping church again.

In the weeks that followed, the principal paid a lot more attention to me than she had prior to my little meltdown. She said good things about me to other members of staff, and publicly praised me for my strong writing skills. It was common knowledge that I was a writer, but my many issues often obscured that fact. The principal (God bless her kind soul) seemed keen to build me back up. She was not one to speak much, and dealing with emotions was certainly not her strong suit, but in her own ways, she showed me a lot of care. She even offered me a bursary to help pay for my school fees. She called me into her office and told me that she was offering me the bursary, not because I needed it (my sister always paid my school fees on time), but because she thought that I needed a morale boost, to help me get over some of "the problems" I was experiencing.

I went to see the counselor as instructed. She was a Kiswahili teacher with no training in counseling. After a few minutes of awkward conversation, I decided that she was not going to be helpful to me. She did not know who I was and had never taught any of my classes. It just felt like a lot of work starting from a place of no common ground, and I don't think either of us had the desire to try. So we exchanged a few meaningless pleasantries and made an unspoken agreement to never speak to each other again.

As luck would have it, I got a different counselor, in the most unexpected way. One evening during prep, I was sitting in class with my desk locker open in front of me. I must have been organizing it, and I didn't notice that the teacher on duty had walked into the room. She walked over to me and as soon as I noticed her, I closed my locker and grabbed a book.

"Hand it over," she demanded, her hand outstretched.
I looked at her, confused.
"Whatever it is you were looking at inside your desk… hand it over," she said.
"I was just getting a book from my locker," I said.

She didn't believe me. She pushed my hand away, opened my locker, searched through it, and pulled out my stash of letters from Oscar. My first instinct was to grab them back, knowing the kind of stuff Oscar and I wrote to each other. But the teacher's eyes were razor sharp and she didn't look like she was in the mood to entertain nonsense. She started to open one and I quickly got up with tears in my eyes.

"I wasn't reading them please," I cried.

She stopped, looked at me piercingly for a moment, then put the letter back in the envelope. My tears continued to flow as I wiped snort from my nose with the back of my hands. She tucked the bunch of letters under her arm and walked out of the classroom.

My deskmate whispered sorry to me as I sat back down. The rest of the class silently went back to whatever they were doing, probably glad that it was me and not them.

It felt like the worst thing that could possibly happen to me at that time. Oscar wrote very beautiful, heartfelt letters, but they were also quite graphic. He didn't hold back in his expression of things nobody outside of the two of us should ever read or hear. Those letters were a sacred safe space for us, and I felt deeply violated when the teacher took them from me.

The worry that this teacher, Mrs. Okello, would read my letters, and possibly share them with other teachers, was killing me. I thought my life in that school was over. How could I possibly face the teachers again after they read those letters? They would definitely never look at me the same, and I would never be able to show my face in public again. I cried so much that I lost my voice.

The next morning, Mrs. Okello called me to her office. I was worried I was going to get suspended. But the moment I walked into her office (she had an office of her own, separate from the staff room, because she was the career counselor), she smiled and offered me a seat. I didn't expect this kindness, because the previous evening when she was grabbing the letters from my locker, she was a totally different person. She was more like the devil herself then, and the woman in front of me that morning was the complete opposite.

"I read your letters," she said gently. "But don't worry, I did not share them with anyone."

Mrs. Okello was a short, slightly chubby woman with a thick, natural afro, and nerdy eyeglasses. Her face seemed like it had significantly softened from the previous night. Maybe she'd had a good breakfast, or had resolved some personal issues that were weighing on her. Either way, she did not look like she was about to throw me to the wolves, so to speak.

Hearing her say she had not shared my letters with other teachers was a huge relief. I started to feel a bit more at ease as I cautiously sat down across from her. I wasn't sure she knew me outside of this specific situation since she did not teach any of my classes, and I was hoping that she did not. My prayer was that we could get this over with as quickly and as painlessly as possible.

"I've heard a lot about you," Mrs. Okello said.
I tensed up. It was probably not good things that she'd heard about me.
"Your teachers say you are smart, but you seem to have some problems."
I didn't know what to say, so I sat there quietly and kept my eyes on the ground.

The next few hours with Mrs. Okello completely changed my perspective, and my life. She took out the letters from her drawers and spread them out on her desk. My tears started to flow. I listened to her recount what she had read in the letters, every last shameful detail. As she spoke, her eyes were firmly on me. She did not at all seem uncomfortable with the conversation, with the things that she had read, or with repeating them back to me. There was no shame or judgment in her voice, only facts.

I could not speak. I was overwhelmed with emotion, and the only thing I could do was look down and cry. Mrs. Okello had gleaned a few details about my family situation from the letters, and she spoke about that too. Unlike most, she did not pity me for being an orphan. Instead, she used that fact to help me realize that I was on a self-destructive path. She was gentle but firm, brutally honest but kind. She told me there was almost a zero percent chance Oscar would marry me like he had repeatedly promised in the letters. He was a top performing student in a national school that produced excellent KCSE (Kenya Certificate of Secondary Education) results every year, and Mrs. Okello said she was willing to bet marriage would not be on his list of priorities for a very long time. I, on the other hand, was an orphan girl, in a provincial school, with average grades, and no plans for the future.

"People like this boy don't marry their teenage girlfriends," she said. "Unless you meet him again ten or fifteen years from now and you are a superstar in some field with a lot of money. Otherwise I can promise you he is going to be very busy building a career for himself. And once he gets that amazing career, which he will most likely get, you would have to be just as successful to even stand a chance with him."

Nobody had ever sat me down to talk to me the way Mrs. Okello did. The things she told me were hard to hear, but she presented them with care, and most importantly, without judgment.

"I want you to take a very honest look at yourself right now; your grades, your emotional state, your future plans… Do you think you are on a path that will lead you to being successful in life? I don't think you have a rich uncle somewhere that will sort you out if you fail your exams, or do you?"

She was right. I was doing poorly all around. I was at the lowest I had ever been in my academic performance. My KCSE exams were fast approaching, and I didn't have a plan at all. I was so far behind that if I did not make drastic and immediate changes, I was sure to fail.

"Let's say you fail your KCSE exams, what will your next step be?"

I did not have an answer. I thought of the house my family lived in and imagined what it would be like to live there for another five or ten years. I could not do it. I needed a way out, and as things stood at the time, I did not have a way out. The path I was on was going to lead me straight to poverty and misery. I needed to go to the university in order to have even the slightest chance of a better life.

I spent a good two or more hours with Mrs. Okello. She told me straight up that I was in a bad place, and definitely not on track to setting myself up for success post high school. She remained matter of fact, even as I continued to cry.

"My dear, whatever it is that you are going through right now," she said, "you need to snap out of it chap chap and get to work. I promise you that your boyfriend is not sitting around right now thinking about you. He is working… working, working. He is working. He is not thinking about you and your problems. Only you can solve your problems, and your best chance is to ensure you go to university."

The talk with Mrs. Okello became one of the most important talks I have ever had in my life. I never spoke to her again after that (not by design, but simply because our paths never crossed again), but in those few hours that I spent with her, she was like the mother figure I never had. She gave me a long and thorough lecture without at any point making me feel unsafe. It was like a push and a hug all at the same time. She did not even have to ask me, I promised her that I was going to break up with Oscar and focus on passing my KCSE exams.

I didn't have to think about it twice. It pained me to have to do it, but my mind was made up the moment I stepped out of Mrs. Okello's office. She gave the letters back to me and as soon as I got back to class, I tore up every single one of them and dumped the pieces in the trash. I wrote Oscar a one pager, stating that I had made the decision to discontinue our relationship so that I could focus on my studies.

The letters came fast and heavy from Oscar. Initially he thought I was kidding, and he said the joke was not funny. Then he thought he had done something wrong, and he begged for forgiveness for whatever it was that he had done. I read his letters, tore them up, and dumped them in the trash. For some reason, I did not at all feel nostalgic about our relationship. I did not feel bad about ignoring his letters. Instead, I felt highly motivated to make something of my life.

Oscar wrote a lot of letters; sad letters, frustrated letters, angry letters, apologetic letters. I read them all, and ignored them all. When he couldn't get a response from me, he shifted his anger to the girl that introduced us, believing that she had incited me to break up with him. The girl was of course upset and frustrated by this, because she had been nothing but supportive of our relationship.

I understood that he was desperate, but something unusual had happened to me, and I did not feel the need to take care of his hurt emotions. Mama, I know I was cruel in the way that I suddenly and mercilessly disconnected from him. After high school, I saw him in Kisumu town once, and he started to walk towards me. I am ashamed to say that I turned around and ran away. I could not face him. Ours was a beautiful love, but I felt like it was either love (which may or may not have worked long term) or a successful future. It was as though one part of me had to completely shut down in order for the other to reawaken. I could not have a soft spot for Oscar and get good grades. I had to choose one, and to me, the choice was not even a choice. Building a future for myself was a necessity.

CHAPTER SIX

Dear Mama,

How is it possible that someone so broken, with such low self esteem, can also think so highly of themselves and their potential? One thing I never lacked, even as I struggled with awkwardness and self doubt, was the deep belief that I could make something meaningful out of my life. I knew there was a fire in me that, if tapped into, could propel me to success. By this time, I had wasted over three years of my time in high school, and I had less than a year to turn things around and get a decent enough grade to get me into a public university. That was the only chance I had at having a decent life, because unless I got into a public university, where the government would pay for my tuition, I would either not study beyond high school, or I would spend years begging people to pay my tuition. There was no job I could get that could afford me a college education. Unlike my brothers, I had inherited nothing from my father. I was very aware of that. Even the house we lived in belonged to one of my brothers, and it was only a matter of time before I would no longer be able to call that place home.

Mama, I'll be very honest with you. I think in a lot of ways, you destroyed my self esteem. You handled me with immense anger, insulted, and beat me on a regular basis. But I also think that despite all that, you planted a seed in me that reminded me when I needed it the most that I was special. I can't say I know exactly what it was, but I think I got some of that belief from the casual way that you treated my good grades. You were never surprised when I came top of my class. I understood the fact that you were not impressed to mean that you, of course, expected me to shine. And so I learned not to be impressed by myself either. Success was an obvious expectation that did not require celebration. At least that is what I told myself, even though I knew there was the real possibility that you simply did not have the strength left to care about my academic performance. Mama, thinking about it now, I realize that over the years, I have not been able to really celebrate myself and my successes. I remain self-effacing and highly critical of myself even when others point out my accomplishments.

I cannot judge you, Mama. Even when I say you may not have cared about my academic performance, I understand now the complexity of your life at the time. I know you were overwhelmed, and there was a disease that was eating at you and killing you in the most painfully excruciating way. I saw how weak and tired you were, but at the time, I thought that was your normal. Even though it was clearly obvious to everyone around you, my young mind could not understand that you were fighting a life and death battle of your own.

When my grades drastically dropped after your death, and

I became more of an average student than a top performing student, I was not bothered. I was on a decline in every other aspect of my life at the time, and so grades did not seem like much of a priority. Besides, nobody cared, and so neither did I. But I never stopped believing that I was capable of more. I knew that if I put in even half the effort that some of my peers did, I would be back at the top. I just could not muster the strength and will to exert myself.

With Oscar gone, and with my newfound determination to succeed, I got to work in my final year of high school. The knowledge that it was possible for me to get the grades I needed for university admission fueled me to approach preparing for my KCSE exams with a sense of calm and confidence. I was already in a fairly good place in some subjects (more due to natural smarts than effort), and although in others, such as Math and the sciences, I was practically in the Intensive Care Unit, I decided I was not going to fail. Failing was not an option. I could afford to get bad grades for three years because nobody cared anyway, but because KCSE was going to determine my future, I had to pass. I was especially terrified of failing you. I still believed you could see me from the afterlife, and I never wanted to have to live with the feeling that I had somehow disappointed you.

Candidate Year

While I was confident in my ability to pass my exams, I still needed a lot of validation. I needed to hear it from other people, and I went out of my way to try and get positive attention from my teachers. I was already top of my class in English and French, without even trying, so I started with those two subjects. I started participating more in class, going above and beyond and doing everything I could to get some approval from the teachers. I needed them to tell me I was smart, to validate me in some way, so I could gain the confidence for other subjects where I wasn't doing as well.

It worked. My English teacher became an instant fan. He was quite tall and dark, and looked like he might have some Sudanese ancestry. He kept to himself most of the time, and did not socialize much with students or with the other teachers. One barely noticed him when he was not on duty, because he did his work quietly and went home. But whenever he was on duty, his voice could be heard booming throughout the school. Everywhere you went, he was there. He was a terrifying man and often beat people up for small mistakes as though they had committed serious crimes. During our daily evening jog, he would follow us with a stick while riding his bicycle and cane anyone that was lagging behind. It was like a military drill. You had to run and be ahead of his bicycle at all times. He was known to threaten students that he was going to beat them up as mercilessly as he would beat a snake. My strategy in previous years had been to stay out of his way as much as possible. But the moment I started putting in effort and shining in his class, we became friends. I discovered that there was a softer side to him, and he was just as human as the rest of us.

I especially loved my writing assignments. As had been the

case with other English teachers throughout my schooling, this teacher praised my writing skills and often asked me to read my composition in front of the class. He even went as far as saying I was a better writer than him, and that he often felt humbled grading my work. That gave me a serious ego boost, and motivated me to work even harder. I had similar luck in my French classes. I understood the concepts easily, and even though the French teacher did not pay me much attention, I admired the fact that he had traveled the world and carried himself with a lot of confidence.

Within a very short amount of time, my English teacher got sick, was hospitalized, and died. It was a shock. He didn't look sick to me the whole time I had known him. One moment he was terrorizing students in school, and the next he was dead. Rumor went around that he died of AIDS. I'd seen people with AIDS in my life, and this teacher did not look anything like them. He was skinny but had a normal amount of flesh on him, unlike the people I had seen dying of AIDS, my own parents included. It was said that he developed an opportunistic disease that killed him very quickly. His final days were humiliating, according to the rumors. He lost his mind and would strip off his clothes and run around the hospital naked, shouting like a mad man.

Mama, I experienced the loss of this beloved teacher through the lens of losing you. I mourned him as a person, because I had grown quite fond of him, but I was also mourning you. His death triggered memories of your suffering in your final days. My teacher lost his mind before the disease overtook him. I wondered what you lost. What did it feel like knowing that you were on your deathbed? Was it scary? Were you angry, disappointed, lonely, worried, helpless? Did you get a chance to make peace with your fate, or did you go out fighting in protest?

We held a memorial service for the teacher at the church. Much as the teacher had been a harsh one, the students mourned him deeply. The choir led the most heartbreaking songs, and people broke down mid-song so that instead of hearing words, one just heard sobs accompanied by the tune of sad drums and *kayambas*.

The service was both heartbreaking and beautiful. Seeing people express their grief in such raw, unfiltered emotion did something to me. I wanted so much to be able to do that for you. Mama, I have had the same feeling at every funeral I have attended since losing you. Any tears I shed, for this teacher or for anyone else's death afterward, were actually tears for you. Every funeral takes me back to yours, and I am able to shed the tears now that I was never able to shed then. Mourning at someone else's funeral provides a safe cover, an assurance that I will not lose myself in grief, that I will be able to dust myself off when it's over and return to the business of living my life. I fear that grieving for you directly might pose the risk of consuming me and taking me to a dark place that I may not be able to return from as easily.

Much of my life through the years has required that I remain in control, and one of my greatest fears is to lose control and let down not only myself but others around me. And so my tears for you remain hidden, coming out only occasionally, disguised as tears for somebody else.

We got a new English teacher. He was a much gentler, quieter soul, and did not harass anyone in or outside of the classroom. Although I did not get to connect with him as much as I had connected with the other teacher, I was still able to draw some motivation from him to help push me to do better in other subjects. He told me that being good in languages set me up nicely to be successful in other subjects. I believed him, and so I threw myself into the humanities to pull my grades up on that front as well.

It was fairly easy to block out everything else and focus on my studies. I didn't have any friends to distract me. The few girls that I could loosely call my friends had no expectations of me. We talked to each other when we saw each other, and that was enough. I didn't have to go hang out with anybody, didn't owe anybody anything, and so I had all the time I needed to do my own work. I hardly ever thought about Oscar anymore. I missed him sometimes, but I wasn't heartbroken.

The only person I was deeply attached to in the few months that I was fighting to get good grades was God. I turned to God and prayed hard, every day. I told God He was the only father I had, and He was the only person that could help me at that point, because I was so far behind, and I needed a miracle to turn things around. The fear of failing my exams was real, but I drowned out that fear with prayer and the strong belief that I was going to succeed. In those few months, I shelved everything else. I did not care what was happening at home, didn't care who was doing what with their lives, I didn't even care about my own pain. All that mattered were the exams, and the grades.

When the Mock KCSE exams came along, I scored the second highest marks in both English and French in the entire region, and placed some impressive grades in all subjects, except for Math and Chemistry. My Biology teacher was impressed, and he told me as much. Earlier that year, he had told me I was doomed to fail when I scored two percent in a major Biology exam. The teachers in that school did not sugar coat things. He'd straight up told me I was going to fail. It felt good to prove him wrong. I came from scoring a two percent to posting one of the highest marks in the school in Biology.

My Mock KCSE scores provided just the boost I needed to push through to my KCSE. I had done exceptionally well in most subjects, and I was confident the same would be true for my KCSE exams. My only problem at that point was that I was still too far behind in Math and Chemistry. Even with stellar performance in every other subject, the scores in those two subjects were dragging down my average. I had not bothered to pay attention to those classes, and doing a personal crash program like I had done with the other subjects was just not possible. Math and Chemistry required a lot of time and focus to understand. They required that I get help, and I didn't have anyone to provide that help. I was the kind of student that studied alone.

I did the best that I could to study. And I also did a lot of internal, spiritual work. As much as I was angry with God for my life circumstances, I also understood that He was all that I truly had. I read the bible a lot, recited bible verses, and constantly reminded myself that I was a child of God, and that I was worthy of success. The call of Jeremiah was of particular interest. I related strongly to the way Jeremiah felt when he was called. He did not feel up to the task. He thought that he was too young, and that he could not speak in front of a crowd. I felt the exact same way. But I kept reciting to myself the words that God told him, "Do not be afraid. I will be with you to see you through."

The candidate year is stressful for everyone. My peers were on edge, I was on edge. Everyone understood how important this exam was for our lives, and so different people coped with that pressure in different ways. One girl decided to cause chaos one evening when a teacher grabbed her letters, much in the same way that Mrs. Okello did mine, and took them with her to the staffroom. This teacher apparently shared the letters with everyone in the staffroom, and they all laughed out loud and made fun of the girl as they read her letters.

Any teenager will tell you that there are few things as humiliating as having your personal, deeply emotional life on display for other people to go through and laugh at. It was even worse for this girl because her letters were not from a boy. They were love letters she had received from a girl in the school, and so the shame was not just hers, but her girlfriend's as well. There was a small group of girls that was known for lesbian relationships, and while this was common knowledge in the student community, it must have been such a serving of juicy gossip for the teachers.

Being ridiculed by a whole staffroom of teachers was more than the girl could handle. She paced angrily around the school crying, and when she couldn't take it any more, she stormed the staffroom and attempted to grab her letters back from the teachers. The teachers laughed at her some more and refused to give her back her letters. They made sarcastic remarks and chased her out of the staffroom. The girl went back to the classroom area and started screaming her lungs out. It was around eight or nine in the night, and everyone was quietly seated in class for night prep. The screams jostled everyone out of their seats, as most of us did not know what was happening.

Naturally, when someone screams so loudly and so agonizingly at night, in a school full of teenagers, the results cannot be good. Before I knew it, everyone was scrambling out of the classroom, a few jumping out of the windows. By the time I got outside, all the lights were off, the school was in pitch darkness, and hundreds of girls were running around the compound screaming.

I asked someone what was happening. They told me that there was a strike, because teachers were mistreating us and reading people's letters. Apparently some girls had been planning a strike, and this girl's screams were just the trigger they needed to activate their plans. As soon as the screaming started, someone went to the main power switch and shut off the electricity, and while the majority of people were just innocently screaming and running around, a small group of girls were throwing stones at classroom windows and breaking things.

Most people were not interested in damaging property. The screaming and running was evil enough for them. One by one the people around me joined the screaming strikers. Even those that didn't know what was happening ran into the darkness screaming. To be honest, Mama, it looked like fun. I couldn't help but join in. I ran around the compound and screamed like a crazy person. I didn't care about the lesbian girls' letters. I didn't even care that Mrs. Okello had read my letters. My experience, while initially distressing, had turned out to be a positive one. I wasn't upset about it at all, and I personally did not feel mistreated by any teachers. So my joining in the strike was purely for fun. It felt good to be able to let out some steam in the midst of the tension of looming national exams.

After a short while of mad screaming and running around, some teachers came with torches to try and contain us. They were walking around shining torches on people's faces and threatening them with dire consequences for this atrocious behavior. We engaged the teachers in cat and mouse games, taunting them and running away. Mama, it was one of the most exciting things I had ever been a part of in that school.

Soon enough the teachers got the lights turned back on, and that marked the end of our short, but intensely crazy strike. Everyone ran back into their classrooms and pretended they had been behind their desks all along.

I had never seen our principal so scared, and so disappointed. In the aftermath of the strike, everyone sat quietly and tried to process what had just happened. We were asked to remain in the classrooms late into the night as the principal and the teachers congregated in the staffroom to figure out a way forward. After a while, the teachers distributed themselves into all classrooms to debrief that incident with us. Of course everyone denied any kind of involvement in the strike, and no one was willing to put anyone else's name out there either. Most of us were shaken by this incident. It was not the kind of thing that happened in our school. As much as I had participated, the feelings I experienced in the aftermath were feelings of shock and fear. I got carried away in the excitement of the moment, but a strike is not something I would have wanted to be associated with.

A number of girls ended up expelled from the school for leading that strike. The principal expressed her disappointment in all of us as a school, but life quickly went back to normal. We resumed our desperate grind in preparation for our KCSE exams, and the incident was soon as good as forgotten.

The exams finally came, and I told myself that I was as ready as I would ever be. I had given it my best effort in the short timeframe that I had, and even though I knew my scores in Math and Chemistry would not be the best, I was okay with that. I just needed to get an average that was good enough to get me to a public university, and I knew I could achieve that.

I was at peace. As a candidate class, we got together every

evening during the month of exams to worship together and encourage each other. We sang songs of praise and prayed, and sometimes a few girls would share scriptures from the bible. It was a very intimate experience, both with God, and with the other candidates.

When the exams were over, we gathered all our books in a pile and lit them on fire. It was a tradition across many schools - a terrible one, but a tradition nonetheless. We called it the "Academic Fire". It was a way of expressing that exhale after years and years of academic pressure, a way to say that we were finally through with the stress of school and were now officially grown-up citizens of the world.

Not a Big Deal

The great exhale after completing secondary education was followed by long days of wondering what next. I slept until there was no more sleep left in my eyes. There was nothing to do at home, so I spent the days just sitting around. I decided to go to Busia, where my brother, Paul, lived with his new wife and child. I had not been there in a long while.

The place looked just about the same as it did when we left; the cypress trees, the rows of houses, the shops, and even some of the same people that lived there eight years before. I was pleased to see that the old man, Etyang, was working for my brother now. He had not aged a day. He still had the same energetic walk, the same laugh, the same exaggerations in his stories, and he wore the same old trench coat when he reported to his watchman duties. He made a fuss about how much I had grown, and spent a whole evening reminiscing about you and the good old days. Seeing him again brought me such happiness.

The place was heavy with your presence. I saw and felt you everywhere. Everytime I went to the little well in front of our old house, I could see you sitting on a mat next to it, staring aimlessly into space. The house was rented out to a young family now, while my brother lived in two of the single room houses behind the shops. Sometimes I watched the little kids living in our old house and wondered if they were having an experience similar to what I had. I wondered if they went to the same school, the same church, if their days were filled with silence too, and their nights with fear. Every memory I had of my childhood was in this place. Mama, sometimes I could sit somewhere and see myself as a seven year old, just walking around that old house. I wanted to reach out and give my younger self a hug, tell her that she would be okay. But I always zapped myself out of it and reminded myself to focus on the present, on the excitement of having completed school, and on the fact that I could now do anything I wanted without having to worry about exams.

Paul seemed to have changed quite a bit. He was not as scary as he used to be. Life, and getting older, seemed to have mellowed him down a little bit. He still drank, but even when he came home from his drinking sprees, he was nice, and tended to just eat, tell some old stories, and go to bed.

I was quite entertained by his stories. He and I seemed to remember our childhoods very differently. He idolized our father, spoke of him as though he was the greatest man to ever live. He spoke of all these grand gestures that our father made, the many things that he accomplished, some of them true, some of them not. I didn't really care about the exaggerations, or the lies. He was basking in fond memories of his father, so who was I to get in the way of that? We were more aligned on the memories of you. He remembered the beatings and the insults. Mama, I also had clear memories of a time that you beat Paul up so badly I got scared. You mostly used small sticks to cane us, but on that occasion, you got a huge stick and gave Paul a terrible beating. I don't remember what he had done wrong, but he definitely got the beating of his life that day. The only other time I had seen someone beaten that badly was during the 1992 general elections when some older boys in school tattooed political writings on their bodies using hot metal. The boys were made to strip down to their underwear and beaten like criminals. I was only about eight years old then, but what I saw taught me to never mess with politics.

Mama, Paul's memories favored our father, and that was okay. I remembered him differently. Rather than dwell on the past, I chose to try and be as present as possible, especially for my little niece, with whom I had developed a special bond. Yes, Paul had a brand new wife. She was a thousand times better than his previous girlfriend. When I first arrived at their house, she got down on her knees to say hello and welcome me. I was confused by this, until I learned that she had some Ugandan roots. The women in Uganda are known for that kind of thing. They kneel down to greet people, or even to serve them food. I liked my new sister-in-law immediately.

This young woman's name was Mercy. She was a petite, slim woman with short, natural hair. Like many Ugandan women, she pulled off the short hair look beautifully since her facial features were perfect for it. She treated me kindly, and made her house homely and welcoming. She cooked and cleaned, and constantly checked in to make sure I was comfortable. Her baby was the first next generation child in our immediate family, and it felt good to be an aunt. It was such a delight having Mercy join our family, especially since she was so nice and nurturing.

It wasn't until her younger sister came to visit that I learned of Mercy's fierce side. Her sister was still in high school, but we were close enough in age that we became fast friends and spent every day doing house chores and chatting together. She told me the story of how my brother got rid of his previous girlfriend and replaced her with Mercy. Paul tricked the woman that he wanted them to go visit her parents in Kisii. The woman was excited because Paul had not formally married her, and so in her mind, going to meet her parents was a positive step towards formalizing their union.

The visit went well. He met her parents, spent some time with them, and generally behaved like a good future son-in-law. When Paul left their home, he told them that he needed to go take care of some business back home, but that she should stay a few more days since she had not seen her parents in a while. He promised to come back for her after a few days.

The woman waited and waited. Paul never came back. Instead, he was busy bringing home a new wife that was already pregnant with his baby. Mercy came into his home, made herself comfortable, and settled all the way in. When the old girlfriend got tired of waiting for Paul to come and get her, she took a bus and came back to a home that she thought was still hers, only to find that it no longer was.

Naturally, a war of words ensued. The first wife was a big woman, a solid full size woman with a stern face and arms that looked like they could throw someone across the room effortlessly. Mercy on the other hand was a petite, heavily pregnant woman. Putting them side by side, they were definitely not a match for a physical fight. They exchanged words, each laying claim to the house and the man, and when the threat of violence became imminent, Mercy unleashed her crazy. She broke a glass bottle and threatened to cut the bigger woman. This featherweight sister-in-law of mine, who knelt down to greet me the first time we met, had a fierce side to her after all. She came at her rival with a broken glass bottle and chased her out of her home. The old girlfriend left, reluctantly giving up the man to the new woman in his life.

Mercy won the battle, but what she did not know was that it was a battle she would have to fight over and over again for years, not with this particular woman, but with a number of other women. According to her sister, she was close to her due date when another woman came to her house looking for Paul. The woman was so confident. She came all the way up to the house and asked to see him. Mercy asked what she wanted. The woman wouldn't say, maintaining that she just wanted to see him. I don't know if Mercy knew this woman, if she knew about any kind of relationship she might have had with Paul, but the whole thing didn't sit right with her. As soon as the woman left, Mercy picked herself up, with her almost due for delivery pregnancy, and followed her. She took a razor blade, ran after her and attacked her, cutting up her face horribly. The woman barely had a chance to defend herself.

According to Mercy's sister, the woman was taken to the hospital and the matter reported to the police. But because their father had some connections with the police, the issue was never pursued.

Hearing all these stories about my sister-in-law made me fear her a little bit. With me she was very gentle and kind, but I gained some new respect for her, and reminded myself never to cross her if I could help it. She was quite old fashioned in the way that she treated my brother. She served his food, washed his hands, and just generally treated him like the king of the house. My brother also appeared to be a calmer version of himself, as though he had gone through some kind of transformation since the last time I saw him. Although sometimes he did give orders to his wife, she took them in stride and for a while during my stay at their house, nothing escalated to a physical altercation.

Until it did. I should have known that the transformation was too good to be true. It was Christmas morning, and by then I'd been with them just over a week. Mercy and I prepared breakfast, and we all happily sat together in the small living room for a family meal. It was the three of us, together with their baby girl, who was only a few months old at that point. A young boy knocked at the door. We invited him in. The boy, about seven or eight years old, came into the house and stood sheepishly at the door. He seemed very uncomfortable. I didn't know who he was, and it seemed like Mercy didn't know him either. To break the awkwardness, we offered him some breakfast. He sat down, ate some breakfast with us, and afterwards just continued sitting there awkwardly.

Mercy and I cleared the dishes and went outside to wash them. She said she suspected something was off, and went back to the house to try and eavesdrop on what the boy was telling my brother. When she came back, she was clearly furious. The boy walked out of the house and started heading out of the compound. Mercy grabbed a big stick and followed him. Before I knew what was happening, she had descended on the poor boy with the stick, beating him mercilessly. Paul, together with a number of neighbors came to the rescue. They grabbed her away from the boy and he ran off crying.

Paul threw Mercy to the ground and started beating her. Because the boy was safely out of harm's way, and it was now a fight between husband and wife, the neighbors retreated. It was not uncommon in that area for husbands to beat their wives.

Generally, other people did not interfere in domestic conflicts. So Paul punched and slapped her a few times, but being the little warrior that she was, Mercy broke free and ran a safe distance away from him. She was crying, shouting, and threatening to leave him with the baby and go back to her parents' house. Paul said nothing, and every time he tried to run towards her to beat her some more, she ran out of reach and continued to yell at him.

This whole time, I was standing at the front of the house holding my niece, a beautiful, calm baby, with the most amazing smile. I thought she looked just like my brother, but with a lighter skin tone and a chubbier face.

Mama, I hated conflict, especially when it got physical. Every time I saw a man being violent to a woman, my heart started to race. I felt helpless in this situation. I could not interfere. I knew my brother was a violent man, and I did not want to get caught up in that. As a younger sibling in our family, I was also conditioned to stand back and let other people deal with things. And so as I watched my brother being violent to my new sister-in-law, even without my paralysis in the face of violence, I did not feel empowered to intervene in any way.

When my brother got tired of chasing his wife around the compound, he went back into the house and lit a cigarette. Just like our father, Paul was a chain smoker. He could barely go an hour without smoking. I hated the smell of it, and would usually go outside when he was smoking in the house. It was a small bedsitter house with a curtain partitioning it into a livingroom and a bedroom. Behind the curtain was a bed where I slept. And next to the house was an identical bedsitter that served as a master bedroom for my brother and his wife. My brother smoked in the living room while I sat outside with the baby. Mercy went into their room, packed some clothes, and yelled that she was leaving. My brother said she could go if she wanted. She took her bag and left.

I was horrified. I sat there with a baby in my arms, knowing very well that there was no way my brother could take care of that baby. And I did not feel like I knew enough about caring for babies to be left in charge of one. But I said nothing. I did not feel like I could say anything given the violence I had just witnessed. As much as possible, I wanted to remain invisible in all this, because I didn't want to risk getting caught up in a potentially dangerous situation.

Barely an hour later, Mercy was back with her bag. She went straight into their room and locked the door. She started wailing in there. The neighbors went to talk to her through the window. Paul ignored her. I just sat there, holding on to their baby, my chest hurting in the familiar way that it did whenever I felt unsafe, and my feet completely weak. I could not do anything.

After a while of this, I heard some neighbors shouting that Mercy was killing herself. So everyone came to the house and was yelling for her to open the door. She wouldn't do it, and she kept saying she had taken some medication and was going to die. Paul came to the window and ordered her to open. Still she wouldn't open the door. She said she wanted to die.

Eventually, after much persuasion from the neighbors, Mercy opened the door. She was taken by bicycle to a clinic. All this while, I was sitting there with her baby, watching the drama unfold and wondering what I was going to do with a baby that little.

Turned out Mercy had overdosed on some pills, but it was probably not that bad because she was back home by evening, bubbly and acting as though nothing had happened. She even prepared dinner for us and served my brother's plate with a smile on her face.

Coincidentally, my sister Lena showed up that same evening. There were no cell phones at the time, so nobody had told her what was happening. She'd just decided to pop in for a visit before traveling to her house in Nairobi the next day. Mercy begged me not to tell Lena what had happened that day.
"These are just normal husband and wife quarrels," she said. "It was no big deal."
I promised not to say anything, but of course there was no way I was going to keep that kind of thing to myself. As soon as the two went to bed, I recounted the whole story to my sister. She was not surprised, but she agreed with me that it was best for me to travel with her when she left for Nairobi the next day.

We spent the day after Christmas with my brother and his wife, then got on the night bus to Nairobi. I had never been to Nairobi before. The prospect of traveling to this big city was exciting. We traveled overnight, and throughout the journey, I was looking out the window, trying to soak in as much of this experience as possible. When we got there, it was still too dark to walk around the city, so we sat at the bus stop booking offices for a while before making our way to the *matatu* stage, where we boarded a *matatu* to my sister's house.

Lena lived at the servant quarters of a maisonette in a gated community. I had never seen a group of houses so well organized before. There was a large main gate manned by a security guard in uniform, and once you got in through the gate, there were neat rows of houses on either side of a paved street, each with a fence and a gate, and little signs with house numbers. The road turned several times, and each turn revealed bigger and more beautiful houses. It was like a totally different world from the one I'd lived in my whole life. This was real living.

To get to my sister's house, we had to walk through her landlord's living room and kitchen, and out through their back door. There was a bathroom to the left, right outside of the main house kitchen, which then connected to Lena's house.

The house was small, a single room with a four by six bed, a small wooden sofa with cushions on it, a coffee table, and a cabinet that had a small TV on it. It was not the massive mansions we had seen on our way there, but to me, compared to where I was coming from, this was perfect.

CHAPTER SEVEN

Dear Mama,

Over the years, I have seen what my sister, Lena, has gone through and what she has had to put up with for the sake of her siblings. It is indeed a lot, and I empathize. And so even as I speak about my experiences with her and my relationship with her, it is not to downplay the important role that she played in our lives. I remember hearing somewhere that you begged her, on your deathbed, to take care of your children. She was only about seventeen or eighteen years old at the time. And this heavy responsibility was put on her shoulders, to take care of five younger siblings. It must have been overwhelming. Where would I even start at that age?

I completely understand why you would put that responsibility on her, Mama. You did what you had to do. God knows my father could not be trusted to be there for the day to day messiness of raising children. Lena was probably the only choice that you had. She had to step up as the eldest of us, and as a mother now, I can imagine how painful it must have been for you to have to hand this responsibility to someone that was still barely out of childhood herself.

Lena took this responsibility seriously. Although she was not often present physically, she made sure that we had money for food, and our school fees were paid every term. It helped that my father left behind some resources to make this possible, but Lena certainly stepped up to manage those resources and make sure that we all got an education. I am indebted to my sister for that.

The thing that Lena struggled with was the human, emotional side of being a big sister. Even now, with all the empathy that I have for everything she has been through, I cannot say that my sister raised me. She paid my school fees, and she made sure we did not starve, but she was not there for my process as I went through the stages of childhood, puberty, and young adulthood. She did not know anything about what was going on in my life, who my friends were, how I was coping with the unusual life we were leading, how I was doing in school. She did not have a clue what I was going through, and she never gave any indication that she might care. I cannot blame her for any of that. She was a child herself, and not many would have been able to step up in the way that she did when we were orphaned. I certainly don't think I would have had the patience to put up with the things that she had to put up with. And so, Mama, none of this is about judgment or blame. It is simply my experience of what it was like living with my sister after high school.

Too Much of Me

Mama, Nairobi was indeed the best place I'd been so far in my life. I couldn't remember the last time I had listened to the radio and watched television consistently, and with so many channels to choose from. We had a TV when my father was alive, but it broke down soon after his death, and ever since, the only way we got to watch TV was if we went to someone else's house. I remember one of our tenants had a TV at some point, and one time he got tired of us going to watch TV at his house, so he practically shut the door in our faces. Once in a while I would pay five shillings to watch a movie at one of those *mabati* shacks at the marketplace that showed loud, unrealistic action films. Surprisingly, the films were quite entertaining.

Watching TV was one of my favorite things about living in Lena's house. She also had a radio, which I listened to in the mornings and evenings; the morning show and the evening drive. I felt such a connection with the radio presenters. I could listen to them all day. One time I emailed one of them and got a response back! She was a sweet, kind, and beautiful woman, and for a while we emailed back and forth. Mama, the internet was not readily available at the time. The first time I even touched a computer was after high school, when I walked into a Cyber Cafe and requested help acquiring an email address. The lady at the Cyber Cafe showed me how to send an email, and how to check my inbox. Going to the Cyber Cafe became one of my favorite things to do. I had my radio presenter penpal, and a boy I was casually dating long distance. He was the brother of one of my old friends from high school, and had recently moved to the US. The whole time he was in Kenya, he never said more than a few words to me, but we met at a Cyber Cafe a few days before he traveled out, and ended up liking each other.

I enjoyed listening to music. Mama, to this day, some of the songs I listened to during that time elicit warm feelings of nostalgia in me. The songs talked to me, touched me to the core. It was like a spiritual experience listening to that music. I felt like I was in a new world, a world of endless possibilities, a world of beauty, music, and confident, sophisticated humans. This was the life that I needed, and I enjoyed it immensely.

As I enjoyed my new life in Nairobi, I failed to notice that I was irritating and suffocating my sister. She barely ever talked to me, but I wasn't worried about her silence because my sister and I did not have much to talk to each other about anyway. We lived together mostly in silence, except for the sound from either the TV or the radio. To me, that arrangement was not a problem at all.

Being a nurse, Lena worked on a rotational schedule; some days she went to work in the morning, some days in the afternoon, and some days she went overnight. I lived for the days she went to work overnight, because on those days, I could watch TV all night, I could cook whatever I wanted, and I could even sleep in her bed. While I grew up sharing a bed with both of my sisters, when I lived with Lena, I had to sleep either on the couch, which was basically a long wooden chair with some cushions on it, or on a mattress on the floor. She had become very particular about not wanting people to touch her stuff. I was okay with that. I slept on the floor, and it was still a hundred times better than sleeping in the snake-infested house at Kisumu. But when my sister went to work overnight, I would sleep in her bed, even though I knew she hated that, and then wake up early and neatly make the bed so she wouldn't know I'd slept in it.

When she came from her overnight shifts, she would usually sleep most of the day. But I noticed that even when she wasn't on a night shift rotation, my sister still slept most of the time she was home. She didn't have any friends, and hardly ever talked to anyone. Sometimes I would speak to her and she would hear me but not answer me. Slowly I became aware that my sister was irritated by my presence in her house. I didn't have any friends around either, and so I spent most of my time in the house. With the passing days, this became more and more uncomfortable. I was clearly not wanted, but I didn't have anywhere else to go.

I loved my life in Nairobi. I loved that I could listen to the radio and know what was happening in the country. I loved that there was electricity, and running water, and an overhead shower with warm water. I liked the feeling of safety, and even when my sister was trying to show me that she wanted me gone, I still preferred to live with that rather than go back home to Kisumu where life was so dark and hopeless.

Did I tell you this, Mama? I passed my KCSE exams! I got a strong overall grade of B. The straight As that I got in my favorite subjects helped pull up the less than impressive grades I got in Math and Chemistry. I was happy, Mama, because I had attained a grade that guaranteed me government sponsorship to a public university. That was all that I needed. I did not waste any time wondering what could have been had I not wasted the first three years of my time in high school. I was content with what I got. The catch though, was that I had to wait two years before I could join university. The same was true for all public university students in the country at the time, because there was a backlog of students waiting to join public universities. I was okay with the wait. I didn't like it, but it was what it was, and so just like the students in the years before us, we got in line and waited our turn. The comfort I had was that my place at the University was guaranteed.

This knowledge that my life was going to get better at some point made me a little too comfortable, and maybe a little too joyful for my sister's liking. She was indeed excited for me when the results came in, and maybe even a little surprised because no one in our family (our extended family even) had yet qualified for a government sponsorship to a public university before.

The excitement wore out for her quickly, and we went back to our silence, which graduated to something of a cold war. I thought that maybe she was upset because I enjoyed watching TV too much, and so I stopped watching, and instead spent most of the time either writing stories in my notebook or just sitting in silence. Trying to shrink myself in this way did not help. She was still irritated. I started going out for walks around the neighborhood. There was a slum area on the other side of this beautiful estate, and they had a marketplace where all kinds of things were sold. I didn't have money to buy anything, but I enjoyed going there to just roam around and watch the hustle and bustle of market life in Nairobi. Sometimes I went to my uncle's house, which was within walking distance of my sister's house.

I grew up not trusting any of my uncles. But when I came to Nairobi, Lena and I went to visit Uncle Momanyi, and I saw that she was comfortable at his house. Somehow, I looked to Lena to learn how to relate with our relatives, and I mirrored her attitude. If she trusted someone, then I trusted them too. Uncle Momanyi was the same Uncle who had stayed with our father at the hospital in his final days. I hadn't seen him in years, and my memories of him were not particularly positive. But Lena seemed to have put the past behind her, and was actually on very good terms with Uncle Momanyi's family. I was happy to mirror that.

Uncle Momanyi's house became a refuge of sorts. When things were thick at Lena's house, I would go to his house and spend some time there, just to give Lena a chance to get over some of the disdain that she seemed to have for me. I didn't feel like I could spend the night at my Uncle's house, even though they made it clear that I was welcome to. I didn't want to impose on them. And so as much as living with Lena was becoming intolerable, I always went back to her house at the end of the day.

One day, Lena woke up early and told me she wanted me gone. She said she would give me transport money, but I needed to get out of her house and go back to Kisumu immediately. She told me to pack up, and that when she got back I should be ready to go. I wasn't surprised. Nothing specific had happened that day to make her angrier than usual, but I could tell she was simply voicing something she had wanted to tell me for a long time. It was obvious that she wanted me out of her house, but I was not going to leave if I could help it. Lena left the house to give me a chance to pack my things. I sat in her house and weighed my options. There was no option involving me leaving that house that made any sense to me. So I chose to ignore her command and go about my day as usual.

Allow me to explain, Mama. I heard Lena very clearly that morning. But Mama, life in Kisumu was impossible. After experiencing life in Nairobi, I didn't feel like I could go back there. I couldn't imagine living in the house in Kisumu again, with the animals on the roof, and the broken windows, and no electricity, and that whole hopeless existence. So as much as it hurt me to know that my sister did not want me in her house, I did not think that going back to Kisumu was an option I was ready to consider.

When Lena came back, she found me outside washing utensils. She angrily grabbed the plates and took them back in the house. She told me not to touch any of her stuff, and that she could wash her own utensils. She wanted me gone immediately. My heart started pounding as soon as she grabbed the dishes I was washing. Violent behavior tended to elicit that reaction from me. For a moment, I didn't know what to do. She came back outside and yelled at me to go pack my stuff. My body went into some kind of paralysis. I couldn't do or say anything. I felt as though my heart would push right out of my chest. The all too familiar chest pains came back with intensity.

Mama, I had never argued with Lena before. I respected her as my big sister and even though we hardly ever spoke to each other (not just while I lived in her house, but even generally throughout our lives), I still thought highly of her. After your passing, she became the person I quietly looked to for direction on how to relate with different people in our extended family. I trusted her instincts, and I respected the fact that she was much older than I was. But that day, Mama, I saw a completely different side of my sister, and for the first time, I tried to stand up to her.

I told her as a matter of fact that I was not leaving. She said it was her house and I was not going to spend another day there.
"Well then you'll have to drag me out of here dead because I'm not leaving," I said.
Lena went into the house, picked up all my stuff and threw it out the door. My clothes, my shoes, my bag. I didn't have much, but she threw everything I owned outside and told me to go away and never come back.

I was heartbroken, but like in most stressful situations I had been in before, I didn't have it in me to cry. It was probably the fear of losing myself in that situation. I couldn't cry because crying would mean I was giving up, that I was helpless, and that I was resigning to going back to a life of hopelessness. Instead I clutched at the only emotional weapon I had that I knew would upset her. For years, my father's family had accused Lena of selling my father's property and using the money on herself. It was something that upset her a lot, and I knew it. So I lashed out and told her to give me my share of my father's money if she wanted me to go away. I told her I would sue her for neglect and for keeping my father's money from me. Saying those things made me feel like I was fighting back, like I wasn't just sitting back and allowing myself to be a victim in that situation.

Mama, Lena was of course very upset about the things I said. But I was not sorry. I told her I wanted her to give me my father's money so that I could get out of her life. Specifically, my father had left some insurance money for myself and my three brothers' education. I said I wanted that money, and my share of the money from anything she had sold that belonged to my father. It was an emotional outburst, a result of weeks of mistreatment that I had endured in my sister's house.

Lena turned around, walked into her house, and locked the door from inside. I was left standing outside, my clothes scattered all over the ground. The landlord's kids and their housegirl were watching us from their kitchen window. I felt ashamed, especially because of the young children watching. I stood there awkwardly for a while, then decided to go, not knowing exactly where I was going. I left all my stuff on the ground and walked away.

It was such an embarrassing exit because I had to pass through the landlord's kitchen and living room on my way out, after they'd just witnessed that whole fight with my sister.

I roamed around aimlessly for a while, and when I got tired, I sat on a bench at a bus stop. Life was busy going on around me - hawkers were shoving their wares in people's faces, little children were clinging on to their mothers as they rushed to some destination, *matatus* were stopping and going, stopping and going. At first I didn't think about anything. I just sat there and observed the rhythm of a city bustling with life. Every now and then a conductor asked if I wanted to board their *matatu* to wherever they were going, and I just shook my head no and continued staring at all the activity happening around me.

As evening drew near, and I got hungrier, I started to contemplate my options. Clearly, Lena did not want me in her house, and trying to go back would most likely result in another fight. I was not ready for that. Kisumu was also not an option I was ready for. Even if I wanted to go to Kisumu at that point, I didn't have any money. I thought about making money, about what I could possibly do to make some money of my own. I was just about to turn eighteen at the time, and as I sat at the bus stop, I thought that maybe instead of going back to Kisumu, I could try looking for any kind of job so that I could move out of Lena's house.

This being Kenya, the job options for a person like me were very limited, especially considering that I didn't know anybody who was in a position to help me find one. The only job I could think of that was possible for me to get at that point was a house maid job. But truth be said, I could not successfully become a maid. I was not lazy, but I had not grown up doing house chores, and I did not know how to do house chores well enough to get paid for it. I could barely wash my own clothes properly, let alone the clothes of an entire family of strangers. The only other option I could think of was to sell my body, which I would do if I wasn't so afraid of disappointing you, and myself. I would probably sleep on the streets and starve before attempting to do something like that.

After concluding that I didn't have many realistic options in the job market at the time, I gathered myself and went to Uncle Momanyi's house. It was getting dark, and his house was the only safe place I knew that would be welcoming.

I was not too surprised to find Lena there. Of course she would come to my uncle's house to try and justify her actions. She knew I would go there, because there was nowhere else for me to go. My uncle sat us both down and gave us a long but gentle lecture about living together in peace as sisters. Lena said she had invited me to her house for a visit, and I had decided to overstay my welcome. I had nothing to say for myself. I could only talk about what had happened that morning with Lena grabbing dishes out of my hands and throwing my clothes out of her house. My uncle kept bringing us back to forgiveness. I did not feel like forgiving anyone, but I agreed to go back to Lena's house, mostly because I did not have a choice. My uncle was very nice and welcoming, but he had his own problems to deal with. Living with him and his family was not an option.

Lena left first, and I followed closely behind, accompanied by one of my younger cousins. I could not imagine existing in the same space alone with Lena, so I requested my uncle to let my little cousin come with us. She was just over ten years old at the time, and she and I were close because she was like the little sister I never had. I was obviously not close with either of my big sisters. We grew up very separate in our experiences and our lives, mostly because we did not have a way of communicating effectively. If something was happening in my life that I felt uncomfortable about, my sisters would be the last people I would tell about it. There seemed to be some kind of shame between us, a fear of judgment, a need to hide our true selves.

I cannot blame my sisters for our lack of connection. We all grew up in the same household where affection was almost taboo. We grew up in conflict, sickness, and depression, so it was not surprising that we kept each other at arm's length. I have no idea how my sisters coped with their realities, but my response to having grown up deprived of love and family support was to crave it desperately. I constantly sought love, connection, and belonging. But never from my family.

When we got to Lena's house, she didn't talk to us. My little cousin and I settled in and slept on the mattress on the floor. We had already had our dinner at my uncle's house. The next morning, Lena woke up, packed a bag, and told my cousin she was going to visit my brother in Busia. She did not say a word to me. There was not a scrap of food in that house, and Lena made sure she did not leave a single coin behind. Noticing what Lena had done, and not wanting my cousin to become aware of it, I took the little girl back home to her parents' house. If I had to starve, I would do it alone, not with someone's child.

The landlord's house maid and I were fairly close. We spent a lot of time together when the family she worked for was out for the day, either at work or at school. She saw what happened between Lena and I, and when I got hungry after Lena left, I went over and confessed to her that I did not have any food to eat. For the next few days until Lena returned, that wonderful young woman served me food at every meal and brought it to me. Even when her boss was around, she made sure to put some food aside for me before serving the family. I was deeply humbled. I had never done anything for her, but this woman went out of her way not only to feed me, but also to encourage me and pray for me. She was an orphan too and had been through many struggles in her life. In fact, compared to her story, mine was a walk in the park. She was worse off than I was, but she was the one holding my hand and reassuring me that things would get better.

When Lena came back, I was finally ready to leave her house. I'd spent the days when she was away reflecting on my experiences living with her, and I came to the conclusion that I was better off going back home, even if that meant co-existing with snakes and other animals. I was deeply hurt that she'd thrown my clothes out of her house, and left me to starve without any money or food. The rejection played into my already existing insecurities around being unwanted and unworthy. And so the moment she got back, I asked her for transport money and left her house, hoping to never have to go back there again.

Belonging

The house in Kisumu was the same shell of a house it had been for years now. The grass and the fence were overgrown. The pit latrine had sunk even more, and was hanging by a thread, ready to collapse into the many years worth of feces at any time and take anyone that stepped on it with them. The tenants in the *mabati* houses no longer used the latrine. Instead they went both number one and two in the bushes right outside our compound. This made approaching the compound painfully unbearable if one was not used to the smell. Arriving back at the house made me want to cry. It was like taking several steps back in life after having experienced a more dignified way to live.

My little brother, Austin, was the only one living there at the time. Bonareri had moved to Eldoret, and Nicco was probably in Uganda at the time. Austin was in form four at the time, doing his best to prepare for his KCSE exams. He was in boarding school for a while but decided that he preferred a day school. That choice might have made sense to him, but looking at the conditions he was living in, I would never have voluntarily given up boarding school to live like that. He was working through his candidate year, alone in a house that felt very much like an abandoned ghost structure.

The house was in a pathetic state. Dirty dishes had stayed in the sink for ages and were covered in overgrown mold. There was a strong stench in the kitchen that filled every room in the house. The house itself had not been cleaned in ages. The hole on the ceiling in my room had expanded and was gaping dangerously, just waiting for a snake to fall through onto the bed underneath. There were bed bugs everywhere, big ones that chewed on you all day and all night long. The bed bugs made my skin crawl. I don't remember them being there in the years prior to this. Maybe my brief stay at Lena's house in Nairobi had made me more aware of the true state of our house. I felt itchy all over my skin just being there. I told Austin I could not sleep in that house.

Luckily, the tenant on the other side of our house had left, and so Austin had moved to a room in that section of the house. The other two rooms in that section were occupied by new tenants. Austin shared a room with a random friend of his that I did not know. But Mama, I was ready to share that small room with the two of them rather than sleep in the main house. The room also had bed bugs, but at least the ceiling was intact. I remember staying up late, curled up on a mattress on the floor, and listening to the two boys snoring. Sometimes Austin would stay up late with a tin lamp, studying for his exams. I felt sorry for him. I knew how stressful being a candidate was, and I couldn't imagine how much worse it was when one had to do it in a day school, with such despicable conditions at home.

I felt safe sleeping in my younger brother's room, but I had to move back to my own room eventually. We didn't have any water at home (usually we bought just enough for drinking, cooking, and occasionally bathing), which is part of the reason our house was so dirty. The other reason was just the fact that nobody had ever made us clean, and so we were mostly comfortable with things as they were. I bought some extra water, cleaned up the house, washed the moldy utensils, put some cardboard and old clothes up to cover the hole in the ceiling, and moved back to the main house. I aired my mattress out every day to try and get rid of the bed bugs, but those guys were not going anywhere. Even catching one was an impossible task. I had to learn to live with them, and soon enough I barely even noticed them. The euphoria of having briefly lived in Nairobi died down, and the condition at home became my normal again.

I found ways to occupy my time at the church. It was a fairly large church led by a controversial Bishop with several scandals attached to his name. He was entertaining though, and he had a bunch of handsome sons and beautiful daughters that kept young people coming. Having been Catholic all my life, it was exciting to attend a church with so much energy and hype for a change. This church had worship music that was invigorating, and the Bishop's daughters were top notch when it came to entertainment. The Bishop had almost ten of his own children, and multiple children in the orphanage that he ran at the church.

Of his own children, most were daughters, and my God, were those girls beautiful! Every Sunday the Bishop's daughters were lined up at the front, dressed in tightly fitting jeans, to dance to the worship songs. It was called *ndombolo ya yesu*. The girls ranged in age from early teenage to their mid twenties. When those girls danced, it was like being transported to an alternate reality where everything was chocolate, curvy, and beautiful.

The church was highly criticized and hated by many in the community. Sometimes when we walked out of the compound, a random person would yell at us and call us prostitutes. I understood that there were scandals associated with the leadership of that church, some serious. I didn't know if any of those allegations were true, and frankly I didn't really care. I was not going to that place for spiritual nourishment. I went there because of my friends, and also because I enjoyed the hype.

The drama group I'd been a part of at the church was no longer as active, so I joined up with a few friends to try and revive it. One of the senior pastors' daughters became my close friend, and we spent a lot of time together, rehearsing plays, hanging out with her brothers, and just talking about stuff. She was about my age, and unlike me, she was highly extroverted. I was happy to just stay in her shadow as she made waves all over the place. I found her to be quite entertaining.

One day this girl told me that she had someone that she thought would be perfect for me. I wasn't looking for a boyfriend, and I very much doubted she had any friends that would appeal to me. The only people she knew that I was even remotely interested in were the Bishop's sons. One was a youth pastor, and the other one led worship. They were absolutely gorgeous, and probably too old for me. They also had a swarm of women after them, so my chances of ever attracting their attention were at almost zero.

The man that my friend had in mind for me was someone that had grown up in the church's orphanage, and now worked for them in some capacity. He was sweet, but nowhere near being my type. First of all the man was short, skinny, and walked as though he could be blown away by the wind at any time. Mama, I understood that the environment in that church put pressure on young people to be seen hooking up with someone, but why did it have to be this desperate puppy for me? The guy followed me around often, trying to make conversation. I had no idea what he was talking about half the time because I was too busy trying to get away from him.

Eventually I made the decision to leave that church. The pastor's daughter kept pressuring me to date the guy, under the subtle threat of cutting me off from the drama group if I did not. Being part of the drama group gave me a sense of purpose and belonging. When I was with my drama friends, the realities of my life at home became slightly more bearable. I obviously did not want to leave, but what had been a source of solace and entertainment became a place where I felt bullied and harassed. Being mostly soft spoken in that context, I chose to walk away rather than endure the relentless pressure. Mama, I was trying to exert myself, to communicate that I did not want that relationship. My friend insisted that I was being snobbish and looking down on the guy because of his background. I am grateful, Mama, that as introverted as I was, my ability to stand my ground and be okay with losing friends because of it, was strong. I knew that being an orphan did not mean that I had to lower my standards, or be a doormat.

Naked Woman on the Grass

After my friendship with the pastor's daughter failed, I went back to spending my days alone in our eerily quiet, bed bug infested house. I was miserable. The days were dreadfully long, the nights even longer. I started hanging out with some of our tenants to pass the time. There was a woman that had three young children and a husband struggling with identity issues. One moment he was a devout Christian, waking up at 3am to pray as loudly and passionately as he could, the next he was Muslim - robes, prayer mats, and all that - and the next a hopeless drunk passed out in his own urine and vomit. His wife became my good friend. She was a village woman that had dropped out of school way too early to get married to the man with an identity crisis. Now that she had three young children and no education, she felt trapped. She would pack her bags and leave every other week, and then come back when she realized life at her father's house was not any better than life with her husband.

Mama, I saw what marriage looked like, and it was not attractive at all. The poor woman got beatings for the most mundane of reasons. On top of that, she had to take care of their children while her husband was roaming the streets making a fool of himself. I saw how excited she got about the smallest amount of money, because she did not have a job and her husband did not make much from his casual laborer work either. Mama, I prayed I would never become so dependent on a man that twenty shillings per day was enough to make me willing to endure abuse and all kinds of foolishness.

One day I was sitting in front of our house when I heard a woman scream. I went outside the gate to check what was happening. There were two men roughing up a young woman next to the row of rental houses that my father built, and that now belonged to my brother, Nicco. I quickly went back into our compound, afraid they would see and attack me too. I watched through the gaps in the live fence, trying to make out what was happening. I knew exactly who the young men were. They'd grown up in the neighborhood, and although they were only slightly older than me, I had never interacted with them. They were the kind of young men that started being thugs early in their lives, drinking illicit brews, taking drugs, and engaging in petty crime. I'd seen them grow from young boys to these out of control young men that were engaging in the drug-induced, public assault of someone's daughter.

They were yelling at her as they slapped and punched her. Apparently, she was the girlfriend of one of the young men, and was being accused of cheating. The men stripped her naked and made her sit down on the grass. They kept kicking her naked body and asking her to confess to the cheating allegations. The woman kept denying that she cheated, and the more she denied it, the more they beat her. They accused her of trying to kill her boyfriend by potentially infecting him with AIDS.

The two men threw that young woman around like a rag doll. They grabbed her by the hair and dragged her on the ground as she kicked and screamed. A few people passed by, but not a single one stopped to help her. Nobody even approached the scene to try and talk the men down. There seemed to be an unspoken rule to never interfere in a fight between lovers. Everyone either watched from afar, or simply minded their own business and kept going.

The young woman lay stark naked on the grass. She was beaten until she no longer had the energy to resist or cry. The men then told her to get up and walk naked to the man she was cheating with's house. She was too weak to get up, let alone walk. They beat her some more and left her there naked, covered only by her own blood.

It was one of the worst things I had ever witnessed, especially since the woman involved was actually just a girl. It left me nauseous, and questioning the meaning of this life. Mama, it seemed to me that everywhere I turned, a woman was being abused. I had on several occasions witnessed neighbors dragging their wives outside and beating them like snakes in front of everyone. Nobody cared. The women were beaten mercilessly, and they all stayed, waiting for the next dose of assault.

Mama, I was nauseated. I was tired. After witnessing that assault of the young naked girl, I decided that I needed to get away from that place. So I packed my bags and went to Bonareri's house in Eldoret. Bonareri had just given birth to a beautiful baby boy. My visit to her house was well timed because I had not met her baby yet, and I was also meeting her husband for the first time.

While Bonareri and I had a lot of arguments through the years, she and I got along better than I ever could with Lena. Bonareri was generally happier and more sociable. She had things to talk about, and when she was unhappy about something, she certainly let you know immediately. With her, I didn't have to guess whether she was upset with me or not. She spoke her mind, sometimes badly, but at least with her, I always knew where I stood.

Life in Eldoret was just as quiet and as slow as it was in Kisumu. Bonareri worked an administrative role at an office nearby. She was on leave when I visited her, so we spent days hanging out at home with her baby, and occasionally going out to the market to buy groceries. She was still as beautiful as ever, and although life had beaten her down a little bit, she maintained a dignified look. Her hair was well kept, her clothes nice and neat, and her house was clean. She had some domestic challenges with her husband, but in front of me, they both treated each other nicely. Her husband was a pastor and had founded a small church where we all went to worship on Sundays.

It was a good life until one day, they got into an argument in the next room, and I heard him hit my sister. My sister started crying quietly, and I screamed. Seemingly, my scream startled them, and they went quiet for a moment. Bonareri then yelled that she was okay, that everything was okay.

Mama, domestic violence, even when it was directed at someone else, was a major trigger for me. It made me either want to kill someone or get away from them. I lost all respect for my brother-in-law the day I heard him hit my sister. I packed my bags and went back to Kisumu. What I didn't know was that my own dose of violence was waiting for me there.

My brother, Nicco, was back in the main house, and he wasn't alone. Like Paul before him, he had decided that it was a good idea to bring home a live-in girlfriend. And this girlfriend of his was a former close friend of mine. I met the girl when we were both still in high school. She was a tenant's sister, and lived in our compound on and off during school holidays. I liked her because she was full of life, and liked some of the same things that I did. We spent a lot of time together, singing songs from the big lyrics book that she had. They used to put song lyrics in the Sunday newspapers those days, and Stacey had dozens of those cut out and stuck in her lyrics books.

I really loved that girl. I thought she was one of the coolest friends I had ever had. What I didn't know was that she was secretly developing a relationship with my brother. I noticed her pulling away from me, spending less and less time with me, and more and more time with my brother. For a long time it didn't even occur to me that they might be dating. In my mind, I didn't really see my brother as someone any of my friends would be interested in. So it came as a shock to me when it finally became clear that I was now the third wheel in that relationship.

I left the girl alone, but being the sentimental person that I was, I wrote her a letter when we went back to school to say how hurt I was that she'd chosen to give up our friendship in order to date my brother. I expected that she would be sorry, maybe even say that she valued our friendship more. But instead, she ignored me, then shared the letter with my brother and told him that I was jealous of their relationship.

So of course I was not happy when I came home and found my former friend living with my brother in our house. She and I were not on speaking terms. Our friendship was completely done, and we could barely stand each other. Things got worse by the day. She started trying to provoke me. She and my brother never cleaned up after themselves. My room was cleaner, and rather than clean their own room, she would come into my room, bathe in my bathroom, use my towel, and walk out without saying a single word to me. Additionally, they would eat the food that I cooked, and leave dirty dishes in the sink for me to wash. The two of them did not cook or do any kind of house chores. They behaved as though they were in a hotel room and I was their maid.

My brother was aware of my issues with his girlfriend, and he stopped talking to me too. I was very frustrated. One day, the girl came into my room and left a mess after using my bathroom. It was the last straw. I walked right up to my brother, who was standing outside, and told him I was tired of his girlfriend's behavior.

It was as though all along, he'd been waiting for me to say something. He did not even wait for me to finish the sentence. I found myself thrown on the ground, with my brother raining blows on me. I was so shocked that for a moment I didn't feel any pain. I felt myself on the ground, with the weight of a man pinning me down, and I could see that he was hitting me. I also saw that some neighbors were watching. I yelled for help, weakly, because I was too stunned to actually produce enough sound out of my mouth. Nobody moved to come and help me. Mama, did you ever have that nightmare where you are in danger but you can neither move nor scream. It's some kind of paralysis where your mind is trying to get you to take action, but your body just won't cooperate. That is what it felt like. In my mind, I was fighting him off, but physically, all I was able to do was curl up as much as I could and protect my face with the length of my arms.

I wondered if I was going to die, if my brother was going to beat me until I bled like the naked woman on the grass, or if he was going to go all the way out and kill me. My mind was racing in a hundred different directions as my brother was beating me. I didn't want to die. I screamed, but the sound got stuck in my throat. I wondered if that was what it felt like to die. I wondered if anyone would come to my rescue, or if they would just watch from afar, the way I did when the two men were beating up the naked woman.

It was over as suddenly as it started. Nicco released his hold on me and walked into the house. I picked myself up and ran out of the compound. I thought it was possible my brother had gone into the house to get a knife so that he could finish me off. So I ran all the way to the shops near the main road. I found a quiet spot on a veranda and sat there for a while, contemplating what had just happened to me.

My heart was still racing, and I couldn't think clearly, so I got up and went to look for a friend that lived down the road from the shops. I'd met this girl and her sister after high school and gotten close to their family. Like me, they were just trying to figure out adult life, and that was our main point of connection. We struggled through the days together and tried to find our footing in the real world. They were also very down to earth.

The sisters were not home. I found their little brother, and just broke down in tears when he told me they weren't there. The young boy looked at me, confused. I turned back and walked away. My tears had been dancing in my eyes the whole way there, and I was disappointed that I did not have anyone around to turn to at that moment. I sat at the shops for a long time. Eventually I saw Nicco and his girlfriend leaving the house. When they were out of sight, I quickly went into the house, got some coins from my room, and went to the shopping center to call another friend.

I went to a phone booth and called an old friend from high school. It was the friend I used to write letters to in our first year, and that chastised me when I got caught writing her a letter in class. Our friendship had suffered many setbacks over the years, but she was one of very few people from high school that I still talked to. I cried bitterly on the phone as I told her what happened. In less than an hour, she was at my house. I had never cried so bitterly in my life. I felt deeply pained, and angry, that this had happened to me. My friend sat with me, comforted me, and reassured me that all would be well.

When my younger brother, Austin, came back home and I told him what had happened, he was very upset. He told me not to worry, that he would deal with it. Austin was a very calm young man, and of all my brothers, he was the one I got along with the best. Being just over a year younger than me, and having grown up without parental support, I imagined he was carrying more in his heart than he ever shared. To date Mama, I have never heard Austin talk about you.

My friend ended up sleeping over at our house that night. Austin also slept in the main house because I was scared Nicco would come back and do something to me. Sometime in the middle of the night, Nicco came back, alone. Austin opened the door, then asked to meet him outside so they could talk. My friend and I watched from a crack in the curtains. We couldn't hear what they were saying, but it didn't take long before Austin punched Nicco in the face. Although Austin was younger, he was more fit, and had been practicing Karate for a while. Physically, Nicco had nothing on him. Nicco took a good beating from our younger brother, and as I watched through the window, some of the bitterness that I felt started to ease. I felt avenged. It was good to see Nicco helpless and wailing like a woman.

The next evening, Nicco came back to the house. After the beating he got from Austin, he'd run off somewhere, and we hadn't seen him since. Austin was at the house with me, so I was not afraid. His Karate skills were all I needed to feel safe around Nicco.

Nicco said he had come to apologize. I was not interested in his apology, and in any case, the apology that he gave did not sound like it was meant for me. He apologized mainly to Austin, and said that it was important that they stick together as brothers. He said that I, being a woman, would one day get married and leave the family, but the two of them would remain brothers forever.

Austin was not interested in whatever he had to say either. He told him to move out of the house and not come back there anymore. Mama, as we grew older, the conversation about property ownership was starting to come up more and more. Everybody knew that the home that we lived in was willed to Austin. Nicco had the houses and shops near the road, and Paul had the estate in Busia. So Austin was within his rights to throw Nicco out of the house.

My relationship with Nicco was completely destroyed by that incident. Mama, I know he is your son, and many people over the years have asked me to forgive him, but of all the things a person could have done to me at that point in my life, physical violence was the worst. It wasn't about the pain, or the humiliation, but rather the trauma that it reawakened in me. All trust was broken, all respect lost, there was nothing left that could form the basis of a reconciliation.

I developed an exaggerated fear of my brother. I was not at any point willing to be within a certain distance of where he was. One time, I was standing near our gate and didn't notice him coming.

When I turned around and saw him coming towards me, I took off screaming. He was startled by my reaction. Whereas he was merely walking to the gate, what I saw when I turned around was a man with the potential to physically hurt me. Because of the tension between him and Austin, I heard that Nicco walked around with a concealed knife. I was not ready to get stabbed, so I was not allowing myself anywhere near him.

Nicco negotiated with Austin to be allowed into the house during the day since he did not have anything where he was staying. Austin agreed to this, but as long as I was in the house alone, I would never let him in. I locked all the doors when Austin was out and stayed hidden in my room. Nicco would knock and knock until he gave up and went away. We didn't speak a word to each other until a few days later when Lena and Uncle Momanyi came by from Nairobi.

Uncle Momanyi called us both to a meeting to try and resolve the issue. Nicco apologized again, but insisted that it was my fault for provoking him. He said I wrote his girlfriend a letter saying I was hurt that she had chosen to date him. That part was true. But then he went ahead and said I had been romantically attracted to this girl, and that is why I did not want her living with him. Hearing him say that was like having salt added to my already painful injury, especially because he said it in front of my uncle. All attempts to reconcile us failed. I swore to Nicco that I would never in my life forgive him.

NO TEARS FOR THE CHERISHED

CHAPTER EIGHT

Dear Mama,

Sometimes I try to put myself in your shoes, to figure out what I would do if my children were fighting and making enemies of each other. In those times, I want to reach out to my siblings and forget everything that happened. I want to bring our families together and have one big celebration. We made it, Mama. We are all alive, and successful in our own different ways. Some of us have fared better than others, but we each have something that we are doing with our lives, and that is worth some gratitude. Sometimes I feel that by remaining aloof to my siblings, I am failing you, and denying you the joy of seeing your children loving and supporting each other through life. That is what I would want for my own children. But Mama, it is not that easy.

For some families, adversity pulls them together, but for our family, the things we endured pulled us apart. We were never willing to talk to each other about our feelings. There was too much shame in that. We pushed each other away to protect our individual dignity; to navigate the messiness of our emotions and our brokenness separately. Home was supposed to be the one place where I felt safe enough to take off my armor, but I absolutely had to put up my strongest defenses there. I felt that it was me against the world. There was no one but me in my corner. I had to fight for myself, and for my own survival. That is why I kept finding myself back in Lena's house, even though she clearly didn't want me there. I did not want to be there either, but I had no choice. My endurance of her cold war was a fight for survival. I knew that one day, I wouldn't have to go there anymore, but until that day came, I had to keep fighting, keep enduring, and working for my own independence.

Over the years, I have tried to make peace with my siblings, with varying degrees of success. There are periods of time when we have been okay, when we have been able to come together and celebrate an occasion as a family. And then there are periods when we all retreat into our own lives and choose to turn a blind eye to each other's situations. In those times, Lena has been the only constant, trying to keep everyone afloat. God bless her for that, Mama, because none of the rest of us has the heart for that kind of labor.

When I feel my grudges against Lena coming up to the surface, I try to remind myself that I probably would not have had the heart, or the desire, to do half the things that she has done for my siblings. I would not have taken as much nonsense from them as she has. While I tend to quickly write people off when they wrong me, she gives them an abundance of chances.

Mama, as much as my experiences living with Lena were mostly negative, I know that she is the one mostly likely to help me (or any of my siblings) should we find ourselves in a fix. I think Lena's problem was one of needing her own space to figure out her own life. Having me constantly in her space was the trigger for all the contempt and hostility that I am still struggling to heal from.

The Decline

Mama, it was 2002, but people were still dying from AIDS, in the exact same way that they died in the early 90s. I was still trying to make peace with the fact that you and my father died from this disease. Even after so many years, I still told people that you died from Tuberculosis. TB seemed like a more respectable disease to die from. HIV/AIDS had a lot of stigma and shame attached to it, and the immediate assumption when someone got it was that they were immoral. I felt the need to shield you, and myself as your daughter, from that stigma.

Mama, one day I went to visit Uncle Momanyi at his house, and what I saw was like reliving my father's final days all over again. It was too familiar, too obvious, and seeing it happen to another relative was disheartening. The man in front of me was a relative I had seen and interacted with often in my childhood. The memory I had of him was of a vibrant, energetic, and hilarious young man. He would make funny jokes and play with us when he visited. It was hard to believe that the skin and bones in front of me was all that was left of this man.

I sat in Uncle Momanyi's house and tried not to stare at my

relative. When he needed to get up, Uncle Momanyi went over and helped him up. It was like deja vu. My mind went back to the hospital room where my father lay in his final days. His flesh had wasted away, just like this man's, and one could almost see life getting ready to slip out of his body. Mama, my feelings about my father were still very conflicted, but thinking about his final decline was painful nonetheless. Being older, I was more aware of the excruciatingly painful process that many people with AIDS were going through on their way to their graves. Whenever I saw someone going through that decline in health, I saw their suffering through the lens of yours and my father's.

Mama, sometimes I am glad that I didn't get to see your dying process as much as I got to see my father's. I saw you weak and depressed, and I saw you sick, but I didn't get to see the bones pushing against your skin. I didn't get to see your flesh waste away until you were left with only a skin-covered skeleton, and eyes that seemed about ready to pop out of their sockets. Part of me wishes that I saw you in your final days, so that I could have a deeper understanding of what you endured, but another part of me is glad that I didn't. Because that way I am able to remember you in a way that is a bit less traumatizing.

Mama, it seemed to me that death was everywhere. Shortly after losing this relative, we lost another one - this time a baby. It was the most painful thing watching a baby deteriorate right in front of our eyes. It made me question the existence of God, and the whole point of life. The poor child was barely a year old, with absolutely no idea what was happening to him. His cry was excruciating. I pitied his mother for having to helplessly endure the knowledge that her baby would not make it. Every agonizing cry must have been like a dagger through her heart.

I tried hard to ignore the suffering around me and focus on getting to the University. The two year wait was tough, especially since there was nothing to do as one waited. I found myself constantly shuffling between our house in Kisumu and Lena's house in Nairobi. There was always something happening in Kisumu that made me feel unsafe, and in Nairobi, I had to learn to live with Lena's mistreatment. She and I never spoke about the time that she threw me out of her house. We seemed to have an unspoken understanding that I was welcome to go to her house if I needed to, but I was not wanted there. She accepted my presence while making it clear through her actions that she would prefer not having me around.

Lena moved to a new servant quarter, and her new landlord was a violent, alcoholic doctor. Mama, I don't think I ever even saw that man's face, but I hated him. Unlike the previous place where Lena lived, we had our own gate and did not have to pass through the landlord's house to leave the compound. I therefore didn't have much opportunity to see the man, but I could hear him clearly through the walls when he was drunk or upset.

He had the most beautiful wife. She was a young mother of a two-year-old, with such a gentle manner and a generous smile. I saw her often because she would come out through the backdoor to do their laundry. She worked at a pharmacy, was clearly well educated, but even she couldn't escape the violence. One time her husband beat her up so badly in the middle of the night and threw her out of the house. Listening to the woman getting beaten was torturous. I worried for her baby, and hoped he was asleep. When her husband threw her out of the house, she stood at their backdoor for a long time, begging him to let her back in. Eventually, she gave up and came to knock at our door. The woman slept on the floor in Lena's house, and the next morning, she picked herself up, showered, put on her makeup, and went to work.

A few days later, she was given several hot slaps early in the morning because she did not wake her husband up in time to avoid getting late to work.

Mama, I wanted to slap that man back. Seeing all this violence made me skeptical about marriage. I could not imagine accepting a life of being physically abused by a man. Mama, I was still so bitter with my brother for assaulting me, and sometimes I wished I could hurt him. My sister-in-law, Paul's wife, was often calling my sisters and I to complain about Paul's violence. We all told her to leave him, but leaving did not seem to be an option she was willing to explore. She stayed and kept enduring the beatings. One time, I visited them and my brother beat her up again in my presence. I took their child outside the house while this was happening and stayed out of their fight. The two of them were always fighting, and I felt sorry for their child, who never chose the trauma that they were subjecting her to. After that incident, I decided to stay away from my brother and his family as much as possible. It was certainly not the first time I had seen him beat his wife, but this time was different. I was older, and I found it extremely disrespectful that he would do that in my presence.

The Hustle

Mama, the two years before I joined University were long and hard, but one bright spot was the friendships that I made. There were two sisters in Kisumu that I spent a lot of time with. They made my days bearable because they could quickly come up with a plan to ensure that we were not bored. Even when they didn't have a plan, they were still great company to hang out with. One of the things I liked best about them was that they were down to earth. They didn't come from a rich or fancy family, so the condition of our house was not a problem for them. I was comfortable having them over, even when there were dishes rotting in the sink and dust all over the surfaces.

The sisters were bold. Sometimes they wore hot pants and crop tops, and walked around the neighborhood like it was totally normal. I would have loved to be able to do that, and even though I was petite enough to pull it off, I did not have the confidence for that kind of thing. My sense of shame was too high. I loved spending time with those girls though. One of them got a working class boyfriend, and rather than ditch us to spend time with her boyfriend, she would bring him home so he could hang out with all of us. Sometimes she would invite us to accompany her to town so her boyfriend could buy all of us lunch.

We also hustled together. We would go to the town center and walk from office to office looking for a job. Everywhere we went, we were turned away right at the door. The only place anyone gave us the time of day was at a bank where the branch manager agreed to meet with us. We told her we were looking for work, any kind of work. She asked us questions about our backgrounds, and our qualifications. Of course we didn't have anything more than our high school certificates. The woman spoke to us with a lot of gentleness and advised that we get some post high school education first before trying to look for a job. She said that even if she wanted to give us a job, there was nothing at the bank that she could offer us. We came out of that place feeling really good about ourselves, even though we did not get a job. The fact that someone had taken time out of their day to listen to us and talk to us was amazing in itself. After being turned away so many times, sometimes rudely, we had not expected that kind of warmth at a bank of all places.

We gave up job hunting and decided to exercise and have fun. We would wake up early in the morning to go jogging around the neighborhood, then spend the day listening to music, dancing, and fantasizing about a future filled with wealth. I had a fancy Walkman that I'd been given by a friend of one of my uncles in Nairobi. It was small but had great sound and could place AM/FM radio and cassettes. It was probably the best thing that I owned at that time. The man that gave it to me had been making subtle passes at me for a while, but I pretended that I did not get it. I entertained him just enough to keep him interested, but never gave any indication that I understood his intentions. I knew that because he was my uncle's friend, it was unlikely he could outright try anything with me.

I was devastated when my Walkman went missing. Several things had been disappearing from the house over the years, and I suspected they were being sold to fund habits that some people in that house had acquired. I was not bothered about people selling stuff before, because none of it belonged to me anyway. But when my Walkman went missing, I was definitely upset. I could not accuse anymore for fear of stirring up conflict, but I went through the whole process of grief for that Walkman. It was the one thing I owned at the time that made me feel connected to the world beyond our house and my friends. I felt closed in, and lonely, and I wanted so badly to get away from that place. I longed for the day I would leave and never come back.

Mama, after what seemed like many years, I finally received my formal University admission letter with a reporting date. I was going to study Education (French). I had hoped to pursue Law, but I was content with what I was offered. Anything would have been okay with me at that point, as long as it meant I could finally leave home and start a life of my own.

The formal admission letter changed my whole mood. I was happier, more hopeful, and not as bothered about the small annoyances that came with living in our house. As luck would have it, one of my neighbors used to tutor some Indian kids, and when she heard I was going to study French, she asked if I was interested in tutoring the kids in French. I jumped on the opportunity, and just like that, I got a hustle tutoring three Indian kids in French.

I had never interacted with an Indian family before. The kids were delightful. They were smart and eager to learn. They inspired me to work hard to make sure that I prepared enough challenging content every day. The parents on the other hand were a different story. They treated me with suspicion, hovering around the room, watching my every move, as though they expected I was up to something fishy. The hovering made me uncomfortable, but when I talked to the lady that found me the job about it, she reassured me that it was normal for Indian families to behave like that around their black employees. I decided to ignore the bizarre behavior and focus on the kids and on getting paid.

The job paid one hundred and fifty shillings per child per hour long session. So at the end of each day, I walked home with four hundred and fifty shillings. Transport cost ten shillings each way, so I was making good money. I was really proud of myself for the ability to work for my own money. Because as a family we generally didn't have a lot of money, my sister, Bonareri, was of the opinion that I should spend some of that money on food. I said no. It was my money and I didn't plan on using any of it to buy food for other people. That created some resentment and a lot of unnecessary arguments. Bonareri had recently moved back home after her marriage ended and she was often in a foul mood.

One night we were sleeping in our room when someone knocked at the door. It had been a while since my incident with Nicco, and over time, he had moved back into the house. From the rude and persistent knocking, it was obvious that it was him. I had made it a rule for myself to never open the door for him. We were still not on talking terms, and I did not care if he slept outside on the grass. Bonareri nudged me to wake up. I ignored her and pretended to be deeply asleep. Her infant son was sleeping on the bed with us, and a new house girl she had hired to help care for her son was on a smaller bed across from us.

Bonareri nudged me again and asked me to go open the door. I said I don't open doors for grown men in the middle of the night. She got upset and she started yelling at me. I was too tired, so I just let her yell and continued sleeping. She pulled the covers off me and said I must go open the door. I stood my ground - I was not going to open the door for anybody at that time of night. The house girl offered to open the door. Bonareri told her not to. She insisted that it had to be me. Mama, I don't know why Bonareri was so angry at me. I had not done anything to her, and she knew that Nicco and I had problems with each other, so I was confused as to why she was pushing this issue. I told her I was never going to open a door for Nicco in my life.

Eventually, the house girl got up and opened the door. That did not sit well with Bonareri. She got ready to fight me. She could not fight me physically. I was not necessarily stronger than her, but I was slightly taller, and I had more fight in me than she did. She however had more mouth and words that cut deep. She proceeded to engage me in a long, exhausting night of insults. I was drained by it, but I decided that I could dish out some of what she was serving too. I gave her a good dose of her own medicine, hitting where I knew it would hurt the most. She called me a slut because I had many male friends, and I called her stupid because she never passed any of her major exams.

We both said the most hurtful things we could think of. I was upset by some of the things she said to me because they were unfair and untrue. She said, for example, that I used to parade myself in front of her ex-husband when I went to visit them. This was both upsetting and hilarious to me. For one thing, at least in my own mind, I had zero sex appeal. I was thin and awkward, with barely any womanly curves. I didn't even attempt to dress nicely. What did I have that I could possibly parade in front of someone's husband?

I took that opportunity to verbally analyze the kind of man that she married. In my opinion, he was a jobless, backward, not in any way attractive wife beater. There was nothing about him that could appeal to me. I told Bonareri that her ex-husband was a loser, and that if I wanted to parade myself in front of men, I would parade myself in front of beggars in the streets before parading myself in front of that lowlife.

Bonareri came at me hard. She was definitely better at the game of insults than I was, and while she was generally vocal, I tended to be more quiet and reserved. She attacked my morality, listing all the men she believed I was sleeping with, and pointing out that I was probably HIV positive. She said I would be dead in three years or less.

I wasn't overly concerned about Bonareri giving me three years or less to live. Unless she was planning to kill me herself. I laughed at her and mocked her intelligence. Throughout her primary and secondary school life, Bonareri was not very book smart, and I rubbed that fact strongly in her face.

In the end, she gave up on the dramatic insults because I was hitting her with facts, calmly and with conviction. The first tears to fall were hers. She got really upset, stopped the insults, and started threatening to kill me. She said she had nothing to lose. She could just kill me and then run away, never to return. Considering how upset and emotional she was, and how far we'd both gone in the terrible things we said to each other, I did not doubt that she could actually do it. In fact, I felt certain that if I slept in the house that night, something bad would happen to me. So I got out of bed, followed by her trail of death threats, and walked away.

I didn't have many choices of places to go at that time of night. I walked over to the *mabati* houses in our compound and knocked on one of the doors. The owner of the house was a middle-aged woman that lived with about five or six children, and a number of adult relatives. She let me in when I explained what had happened with my sister, and set a place for me on the floor along with her incredibly large family. The room was dark. I could feel that there were a lot of people inside, but I could not see anything. The woman gave me a thin blanket and went back to her own corner of the room to sleep.

I could not sleep that night. I was too worried about my sister's threats. Even if she did not do anything to me tonight, I was worried she still might the next night, or the next time she got the opportunity. It was clear that I had touched a raw nerve with her, and she was wounded. She had upset me too, but I didn't take much of what she said to heart since it was not true. I would have forgotten all about the argument had she not threatened to kill me.

The next morning I woke up and went into town. I called my old penpal friend from primary school that I exchanged letters with before I met Oscar. She was a close friend at the time, and I thought she might be able to help. After I told her about the fight with my sister, she invited me to stay at their house until things cooled down. Her mother knew me fairly well, and my friend believed it would be okay for me to stay with them a few days. I went over and spent the day hanging out with her and her older sister. In the evening, my friend's mum came back from work, and while she was generally nice and welcoming, I felt a bit of tension in the house. We sat down for a quiet dinner, then I was informed that I would be sleeping in the guest room. Her mother gave me clean sheets, pajamas, and a towel, and asked if I needed anything else. She was very nice, but it felt like she was treating me with a level of formality not meant for a close friend. I understood the formality to mean that I should leave as soon as possible.

I slept in the guest room while my friend and her sister slept in their room. I had hoped for a sleepover kind of situation where we would sit up late into the night telling stories and laughing. That did not happen. In the morning I was offered a warm bucket of water for bathing, and a nice breakfast. As soon as I finished breakfast, I announced that I had decided to go back home. My friend's mother did not make any attempt to try and stop me. She smiled and thanked me for visiting them.

I wasn't ready to go back home. I truly believed that Bonareri could do something to hurt me. Mama, I see now that I had learned to mistrust everyone, including my own family, when it came to my personal safety. I was constantly in self-preservation mode, and any threat to my personal safety elicited a fight or flight response. I called my sister, Lena, and told her I needed to come to Nairobi. I explained to her what happened, and she said it was a small argument that we would both get over in no time. She reassured me that Bonareri was not capable of hurting me. Either way, I decided I was not going to wait around to find out. So I got on the next available bus and traveled to Nairobi.

All Things Aligned

Mama, the day I joined the University was one of the happiest days of my life. It was like a big exhale after years of struggle. The University was a whole new world. I felt like I was finally standing on my own two feet. I was taking care of my own living expenses, and that was a very meaningful step for me. In addition to the tuition scholarship from the government, I was offered a good amount of upkeep loan by the Higher Education Loans Board, and an additional grant by virtue of being an orphan. The loan was repayable after graduation, but I was not worried about it. In other words, I was set. I did not need a single cent from my family anymore. The only thing I needed was a place to stay during the short breaks in between semesters.

Luckily, one of the closest friends I made in my first year got elected into a student leadership position. Being a student leader meant that she did not have to share a room with anyone, and that during breaks, she could remain on campus if she wanted to. That was a blessing for me because the friend was willing to put me up during breaks. I stayed with her, and only occasionally showed up at Lena's house. Additionally, one of my uncles got me a job (for the longer school breaks) working for a radio station that served a refugee camp in Tanzania. I recorded radio lessons for high school students, and also wrote and printed newsletters for the company.

Mama, I gained some independence, which was exactly what I needed. It was like a deep sigh of relief after years and years of carrying so much anxiety, fear, and shame. I finally felt like I was living for myself, like I didn't owe anybody anything. I was no longer afraid that somebody would beat me up, or try to kill me, or throw me out of their house. I knew that from this point on, no matter what happened, I would be okay.

Mama, I cannot say that life after joining the university was easy, but I was certainly highly blessed. My confidence grew. I had a sense of direction, and I understood that my life was mine to make or break. Although I remained quite reserved and highly introverted, I was not sad. I had many good friends that I spoke to and hung out with when I needed to. I got involved in a number of projects that helped build my portfolio. Life was good, Mama. A friend of mine often told me that you and my father must be really great guardian angels, because a lot of things lined themselves up seamlessly for me over the years. Of course there were many rough patches, a lot of struggles, but in the end everything always worked out for the best, beyond my wildest expectations.

Similar to high school, I spent a lot of time at the university writing stories, and I knew that I wanted to pursue my passion for writing in some way. I talked to people, attended writers' seminars, and prayed. Writing stories was therapy for me, but I was also deeply convinced that it would be my ticket to a better life.

The writers' seminars were important to me. I attended them as often as I could, even though they cost money, which I did not always have enough of. One time, I needed to attend a seminar, but I did not have the money for it. It was during one of those breaks and I was at Lena's house. I asked her if I could borrow some money and she said no. Lena was very matter of fact, and very firm, in the decisions that she made. There was no point begging her. But I felt desperate about attending that seminar. My mind went into scheming mode, and I told Lena that I wanted to go to Kisumu. Getting me out of her house was always music to her ears, so she quickly gave me some money to book a bus ticket so I could leave first thing the next morning.

In the morning, I pretended to be getting ready to leave, but as soon as Lena left for work, I took the money and went to the writers' seminar. I'd already missed a full day because I didn't have the registration fees, but I was glad to be able to catch the remaining sessions.

When I got back home that evening, Lena was shocked to see me. I expected that, and I walked in defiantly, bracing myself for a fight. I explained that I needed the money to register for the seminar, and that's why I had lied to her. She was furious. I was used to her not wanting me in her house, and I was no longer afraid of her. She asked me for her money back. I told her that I did not have it, and when I saw that she was overly upset, I walked out, went to Uncle Momanyi's house and spent the night there.

Mama, upsetting Lena to get that money ended up being worthwhile. I met a college professor from a university in New York at the seminar, and he changed my life. He was an elderly man with long dreadlocked hair and a bushy beard. I noticed that he spoke powerfully, but when he wasn't speaking, he was dozing off somewhere. I felt an instant connection with him, almost at a spiritual level. There was no explanation for it. I felt like I needed to talk to him, and as much as I was afraid, the pull was too intense. I walked up to this man and said hello. I did not know what I was planning on talking to him about, but as soon as I opened my mouth, the conversation just flowed.

I asked if he could spare some time to read my unfinished manuscript, which I walked around with whenever I knew I was going to be around writers. It was a novel that I was working on. He read through it quietly for a few minutes, then asked if I could write short stories. I said yes, I could. He told me to write two short stories and apply to the Master of Fine Arts programs at a university in the USA. This man did not know me at all, and he had absolutely nothing to gain from talking to me, let alone helping me. I was this thin, awkward, painfully quiet girl that was easy to ignore. But he not only paid me some attention, but took the time to read my manuscript, and instantly change my life.

Mama, everything happened so fast. Before I could wrap my mind around what was happening, I had a fully funded fellowship to study Creative Writing at a university in New York. At first, nobody believed me when I told them. I was simultaneously completing my final undergraduate semester and getting ready to fly out of the country for my Masters program. I practically finished my final undergraduate exam and got on a plane to New York a couple of days later.

The blessings were lined up for me, Mama. I completed my Masters program without a hitch, and got into a fully funded PhD program without skipping a beat. I was overwhelmed, in the happiest way, by these happenings, and I knew that it had to be you watching over me. Thank you, Mama, for lining up my path with blessings. Thank you for leveling mountains, and walking before me to clear my path. I lost you in this physical world, but I believe that we are still deeply connected, and that you continue to be my angel from beyond the grave.

The Healing Storm

Mama, I met a man - someone that came into my life at the perfect time, loved me with all my flaws, and married me. Can you believe that I met this man within a few days of arriving in America? An old friend that lived in New York invited me to a house party hosted by a Kenyan, and that Kenyan turned out to be my future husband. Prior to attending the party, I'd heard a lot of good things about him from my friend, and so I already knew that I wanted to get to know him. The email invitation said it was a potluck kind of party, so I made some *mandazi* and took it with me.

The man greeted us at the door. Our eyes locked for a quick second, but being the shy woman that I was, I quickly looked away. However, I made a point of spending excessive amounts of time hanging around him at the party, and then emailed him the next day to say thank you and ask if I could get back a bowl I had accidentally left at his place. He emailed back asking for my address, and if he could show me around town, since I was new in the US. I immediately said yes.

Mama, Luka and I were engaged to be married five months after we met. He was just exactly what I needed. He had a very calm temperament, was reasonable and level-headed, and did not have a violent bone in him. He has far exceeded the expectations that I had for what a marriage would look like. Mama, every man in my life growing up was either a wife beater, an alcoholic, an arrogant narcissist, a cheater, a deadbeat, or all of the above. To be honest, Mama, I did not expect that the man I married would be much different from the other men in my life. I hoped he would be different, of course, but I did not really think it was possible.

When I met Luka I was twenty three years old, and he was only a year older. I was terrified at the prospects of getting married so young. I kept thinking that maybe he was pretending to be good, maybe he would change on me and become like every other man that I knew. Mama, I remember calling all my friends and asking them if I was making a mistake. I was looking for validation, for someone to tell me that it was okay to get married. Most of my friends were not yet married, so some told me to wait a little bit longer so I could establish myself financially, and some told me to go for it because there will never be a perfect time to get married.

With my family though, I never asked for validation, because I did not want anyone thinking that I did not know what I was doing. With them, I waited until my nerves were calm, then I told them, as a matter of fact, that I was getting married.

Mama, it's been fifteen years so far since I tied the knot, and I could not be happier with the decision that I made. Luka's calm composure has greatly complimented my anxiety and restlessness. He keeps me grounded and centered. I feel safe, Mama. Naturally, one of my biggest fears when I made the decision to get married was that my husband would turn out to be like my father. I was afraid that maybe I was rushing into marriage because of my need for connection. I did feel very much alone in the world at that point in my life, especially being all the way in a foreign country, very much disconnected from everyone. I was afraid I would get married to fill that gap, then regret it later.

Luka understood my background and my fears, and constantly proved himself to be a man totally different from my father. He found me when I was still in survival mode, broken and skeptical, and my default at the time was fight or flight. In our first year of marriage, I fought him hard. I was constantly looking for issues and provoking him, subconsciously trying to see if he would react violently. I threatened divorce every other day for the pettiest of reasons. Mama, my husband remained calm throughout that stormy phase of our marriage, when I was trying to learn how to trust again, and he never even raised his voice at me. Eventually, I came out of that place of doubt, and I was convinced that he really was a good man.

Mama, we have three children together - your beautiful grandchildren. I named my only daughter after you. Although my husband's traditions dictated that I name her after his mother, we reached a compromise that we would name her after both of our mothers. I needed to honor you in that way. My children are a constant reminder of all the work that you put into raising me for as long as you could. I understand now that it was not easy. And I want you to know that I turned out okay. I still have some scars, but I am okay. I have a family life that's healthier than anything I could have dreamed possible for someone like me.

I accept though that some of the struggles from the childhood trauma will probably be lifelong. Even with a loving husband, beautiful children, a great job, and everything else that I have been blessed with, I still have a lot of fear and insecurities. My therapist said it is the fear of not being enough, and that I need to constantly go back to the little child in me and interrogate the instances in my childhood that led to the development of this self-defeating notion that I am not good enough for the blessings in my life.

Through the process of writing you this letter, I have come to the realization that my childhood still plays a big role in my current emotional struggles. Again, Mama, I do not blame you for any of it. Rather, I see it as my responsibility to work through the mess and learn more empowering truths about myself. I am thankful that I am able to write you this letter, and walk this journey of exploration, understanding, and healing with you. Sometimes I do feel like that little girl again. Sometimes I am that delicate little flower you bled on while lost in your own pain, with layers and layers of fragile beauty, surrounded by self-imposed thorns, and deeply in need of connection. I go by your mother's name now - Nyaboke - because I want to draw ancestral strength from my grandmother, whom you named me after, and other strong ancestors whose blood continues to run through my veins.

Mama, recently I had a bad experience with a close friend, and it left me momentarily disoriented. Maybe because I was in the thick of writing you this letter, I felt the overwhelming need for something or someone familiar and homely that would bring me closer to you. You know that feeling when things are rough and one just needs their Mother? I experience that often. Some days I crave your embrace, I crave your presence in my life, I crave the safety and confidence that comes with knowing one's mother is around, and that they know what to do, and they have the ability to make things that little bit better. I crave the idea of having a mother. I felt that need strongly when my friendship with this person crumbled. So I decided to make a trip to Busia to see what I could find there that might, however mildly, resemble a mother's embrace.

I took a Safety First bus from Nairobi, alone, because the struggle I was experiencing was a deeply personal one. The ten-hour bus ride took me back many years. It reminded me of the many trips I used to make, moving from house to house, seeking safety, when I used to fight with one sibling after the other. That was a time when I did not have a place to belong, and everywhere I went, I was either not safe or not wanted.

You'll be pleased to know, Mama, that I haven't fought much with my siblings since we all grew up and became independent.

On the other hand though, we have not been able to heal some of the old grudges, and so most of our relationships with each other are quite superficial. Some of us chat once in a while, but coming together as a family has been challenging. There are too many unresolved conflicts, lingering hurts and traumas. Maybe this is as good as it will ever be. We are not as close as one would hope to be with their siblings, but at least we are not fighting or interfering with each other's lives.

The bus passed by the hospital where you died. I was overwhelmed seeing that place again. I hadn't been to that part of the country in over fifteen years. So seeing the hospital, with all those people walking around gave me some chills. I felt a connection to that space. If I could, I would have stopped for a minute to get off the bus and step on the ground in the hospital compound. I would have gone in, and asked to see the private ward wing, where you spent your final days. I wondered if your spirit lingered in the air around the hospital after you died, before transitioning to the other side. I wanted to breathe in the air around that place. I wanted to feel your presence, and connect with you, even just for a moment.

The Safety First bus sped past the hospital, oblivious to how much that space meant to me. Soon we arrived in Busia. The place looked very different from how I remembered it. There were many more shops. My old primary school looked pretty much the same, except now there was a new gate, and a secondary school right next door. I almost missed the turn to our old estate. The cypress trees were gone. Those tall, majestic trees that defined the personality of that beautiful path were nowhere in sight. In some ways, no longer having those cypress trees made the finality of your absence so much more real. This was a new place. It was as though my old home had been erased from existence, and what was left was a poor imitation that could never match up to the memories that I had stored in my heart.

It was late. I went to Paul's house, where my sister-in-law prepared a nice meal for me and told me stories about all the things that had changed in that place. She had two more children now, and my little niece, the one I'd held as a baby many years before, was now a young woman, almost out of high school. My brother had changed a great deal too. He was so much more settled and laid back, and he seemed to have found some kind of personal peace. I was happy to see that in him. I was there trying to find peace too, and I hoped that somehow, being in that space would bring some kind of comfort to my soul.

The next day, my sister-in-law and I went out to explore the town. I saw my old nursery school, and the clinic my siblings and I once ran to for help when you vomited chunky blood. Seeing those places was both beautiful and painful. The buildings were now dwarfed by newer, bigger buildings all around them. And a lot of strangers hustling on the streets. I wanted to go into each of the old familiar buildings, but I dared not. My sister-in-law, Mercy, had no idea the journey I was on, and I did not want to share what was going on inside me, lest I fall apart in her presence.

The moment we got back home, the skies opened up. Mama, according to Mercy, they hadn't had a drop of rain in those parts for months. She was surprised when the first drops came through, and suddenly, there were torrents of rain falling violently from the skies. I must have let my emotional guard down because Mercy quickly went into her bedroom and gave me some space. I stood at the living room window, taking in the sounds. With every passing second, the downpour became louder and heavier. It was almost like a protest, like decades of hurt and pain finally finding an outlet, like the violent sobs of a tormented spirit.

Tears flowed freely down my face. I reached out the window and touched the rain. I felt you in that rain, told you that it was okay, that I was okay. Mama, I am sorry that I have carried you so heavily in my heart for so long. I hope you know that I have nothing but desperate love for you. I continuously seek you out, not because I am not okay, and not because I in any way feel wronged by you, but because I need to go through my process of grief for you before I can let you go. I was never able to mourn you as a child, or even as an adult, until now. Maybe I will never be able to mourn you by wailing and being out of control, the way we Africans traditionally mourn our dead. Maybe writing you this letter is my way of grieving, and finally making peace with my past.

You did good, Mama. You did your best. You raised me the best way you could given the circumstances, for as long as you could. I know that if it were up to you, you would have lived longer, and we would have found a healthy rhythm in our relationship. But you did not get the benefit of time. I hope that you can feel the love and gratitude that I have for you. I hope you are at peace, knowing that your children are okay. I release you from any pain, guilt, or hurt that you might have felt having to transition to the afterlife, leaving your young children behind. You did not want that. I know that you fought hard, and that it broke your heart to have to go.

You will forever remain a part of me. I celebrate you and your life. I acknowledge your strength and courage in the face of impossible odds. You were the stunningly beautiful, smart, loving, and joyful woman that my father pursued relentlessly for years, only to turn around and become your demise. I choose to embrace you for who you truly were before life broke you down. You wanted to have a happy life, just like everyone else, and be able to raise happy and healthy children. Mama, you did everything that you could for us. I will do my best to heal, and remember that I am enough. You were enough, Mama. We have always been more than enough.

My love always,
Nyaboke

Printed by Amazon Italia Logistica S.r.l.
Torrazza Piemonte (TO), Italy